Exam Ref Microsoft Security, Compliance, and Identity Fundamentals

Second Edition

Yuri Diogenes
Nicholas DiCola
Mark Morowczynski
Kevin McKinnerney

T0073880

Exam Ref SC-900 Microsoft Security, Compliance, and Identity Fundamentals, Second Edition

Published with the authorization of Microsoft Corporation by Pearson Education, Inc.

ISBN-13: 978-0-13-836373-4
ISBN-10: 0-13-836373-0

Library of Congress Control Number: 2024932891

1 2024

TRADEMARKS

WARNING AND DISCLAIMER

SPECIAL SALES

For information about buying this title in bulk quantities, or for special sales opportunities (which may include electronic versions; custom cover designs; and content particular to your business, training goals, marketing focus, or branding interests), please contact our corporate sales department at corpsales@pearsoned.com or (800) 382-3419.

For government sales inquiries, please contact governmentsales@pearsoned.com.

For questions about sales outside the U.S., please contact intlcs@pearson.com.

CREDITS

EDITOR-IN-CHIEF
Brett Bartow

EXECUTIVE EDITOR
Loretta Yates

ASSOCIATE EDITOR
Shourav Bose

DEVELOPMENT EDITOR
Rick Kughen

MANAGING EDITOR
Sandra Schroeder

PROJECT EDITOR
Tracey Croom

COPY EDITOR
Rick Kughen

INDEXER
Timothy Wright

PROOFREADER
Charlotte Kughen

TECHNICAL EDITOR
Mike Martin

EDITORIAL ASSISTANT
Cindy Teeters

INTERIOR DESIGNER
codeMantra

COVER DESIGNER
Twist Creative, Seattle

COMPOSITOR
codeMantra

GRAPHICS
codeMantra

Contents at a glance

Contents

Acknowledgments

The authors would like to thank Loretta Yates and the entire Microsoft Press/Pearson team for their support in this project and Mark Simos for reviewing the book.

Yuri: I would also like to thank my wife and daughters for their endless support; my great God for giving me strength and guiding my path on each step of the way; my great friends and coauthors Nicholas DiCola, Kevin McKinnerney, and Mark Morowczynski for this amazing partnership. My manager, Rebecca, for always encouraging me to achieve more and stretch myself to the next level. Thanks to the support from our learning team, especially Cecilia Perez-Benitoa for her contribution to this project. Last but not least, thanks to my parents for working hard to give me an education, which is the foundation I use every day to keep moving forward in my career.

Nicholas: I would like to thank my wife and three children for supporting me while working on this book and my coauthors and friends, Yuri, Kevin, and Mark, for their hard work on this book. I would also like to thank our engineering teams and technical reviewers for their support during the production of this book.

Kevin: I would like to thank my wife and daughter for always being with me and supporting me in everything I do; my parents for their love and support throughout my life and showing me that I can accomplish anything I set my mind to; and my coauthors Yuri, Nick, and Mark for inviting me along on this journey. I would also like to thank all my information protection CXE teammates for their knowledge and mentorship throughout the years. I would not be here today without the help you have provided me.

Mark: I would like to thank my parents for being the most loving parents anyone could have asked for. I would not be where I am today without them. I'd also like to thank my grandma, who I've been extremely lucky to have in my life for too many reasons to name. Thanks to my brother, who is always in my corner and the best fantasy baseball comanager. Thanks to my girlfriend, who listened to me complain through the entire writing process and was way more supportive than I would have been. Thanks to all my coworkers over the years who have spent the time to help me improve in my career. I can never thank you all enough, and I hope this book will help our readers, if even by a fraction of the amount that you all have helped me.

About the authors

YURI DIOGENES, MSC

Yuri has a Master of Science in cybersecurity intelligence and forensics investigation from UTICA College and is currently working on his PhD in Cybersecurity Leadership from Capitol Technology University. Yuri has been working at Microsoft since 2006; currently, he is a Principal PM Manager for the Customer Experience Engineering Defender for Cloud Team, where he manages a global team of product managers focusing on cloud security posture management and workload protection. Yuri has published more than 30 books, mostly about information security and Microsoft technologies. Yuri is also a professor at EC-Council University, teaching in the Bachelor in Cybersecurity Program. Yuri has an MBA and many IT/security industry certifications, such as CISSP, MITRE ATT&CK® Cyber Threat Intelligence Certified, E|CND, E|CEH, E|CTI, E|CSA, E|CHFI, CompTIA Security+, CySA+, Network+, CASP, and CyberSec First Responder. You can follow Yuri on Twitter at @yuridiogenes.

NICHOLAS DICOLA

Nicholas is a Security Jedi and the VP of Customers at Zero Networks, where he leads a global team responsible for all things customer related. He has a Master of Business Administration with a concentration in information systems and various industry certifications such as CISSP and CEH. You can follow Nicholas on Twitter at @mastersecjedi.

KEVIN MCKINNERNEY

Kevin is a senior program manager on the Microsoft Purview Data Governance Customer Experience Engineering (CxE) Team, where he provides best practices and deployment guidance to help customers quickly onboard the Microsoft Purview Data Governance solution. Kevin has been working at Microsoft since 2011 in various roles, including senior support escalation engineer on the Microsoft CSS Security team and senior premier field engineer, focusing on Microsoft security and information protection. Kevin has authored dozens of blog posts and videos related to information protection and Purview data governance and has spoken at many technical conferences, including RSAC, Microsoft Ignite, Microsoft MVP Summits, and the Microsoft Security Engineering Advisory Council. Prior to starting at Microsoft, he worked for IBM as a Microsoft support manager and spent eight years as an information systems technician while on active duty in the United States Navy. Kevin received a Bachelor of Science in business management from the University of Phoenix and holds many certifications, including CISSP and GCIH. You can follow Kevin on Twitter @KemckinnMSFT and on GitHub (*github.com/kemckinnmsft*).

MARK MOROWCZYNSKI

Mark Morowczynski is a principal product manager on the Security Customer Experience Engineering (CxE) team at Microsoft. He spends most of his time working with customers on their deployments in the Identity and Access Management (IAM) and information security space. He's spoken at various industry events such as Black Hat, Defcon Blue Team Village, Blue Team Con, Microsoft Ignite, and several BSides and SANS Security Summits, to name a few. He has a BS in Computer Science and a MS in Computer Information and Network Security as well as an MBA from DePaul University. He also has an MS in Information Security Engineering from the SANS Technology Institute. He can be found online on Mastodon @markmorow@infosec .exchange or on his website at *https://markmorow.com*.

Introduction

The SC-900 exam is targeted at those looking to familiarize themselves with the fundamentals of security, compliance, and identity (SCI) across cloud-based and related Microsoft services. This exam is targeted at a broad audience that includes business stakeholders, new or existing IT professionals, or students interested in Microsoft security, compliance, and identity solutions. This exam covers topics such as Microsoft Azure and Microsoft 365 and requires you to understand how Microsoft security, compliance, and identity solutions can span across these areas to provide a holistic and end-to-end solution.

This book covers every major topic area on the exam but does not cover every exam question. Only the Microsoft exam team has access to the exam questions, and Microsoft regularly adds new questions to the exam, making it impossible to cover specific questions. You should consider this book a supplement to your relevant real-world experience and other study materials. If you encounter a topic in this book that you do not feel completely comfortable with, use the "Need more review?" links you'll find in the text to find more information. Be sure to research and study these topics. Great information is available on docs.microsoft.com, MS Learn, and in blogs and forums.

Organization of this book

This book is organized by the "Skills Measured" list published for the exam. The "Skills measured" list is available for each exam on the Microsoft Learn website: *learn.microsoft.com/en-us/training/*. Each chapter in this book corresponds to a major topic area in the list, and the technical tasks in each topic area determine that chapter's organization. For example, if an exam covers six major topic areas, the book will contain six chapters.

Preparing for the exam

Microsoft certification exams are a great way to build your resume and let the world know about your level of expertise. Certification exams validate your on-the-job experience and product knowledge. Although there is no substitute for on-the-job experience, preparation through study and hands-on practice can help you prepare for the exam. This book is not designed to teach you new skills.

We recommend augmenting your exam preparation plan by using a combination of available study materials and courses. For example, you might use the Exam Ref and another study guide for your "at-home" preparation and take a Microsoft Official Curriculum course for the classroom experience. Choose the combination that you think works best for you. Learn more about available classroom training and find free online courses and live events at *microsoft.com/learn*. Microsoft official practice tests are available for many exams at *aka.ms/practicetests*.

Note that this *Exam Ref* is based on publicly available information about the exam and the authors' experience. To safeguard the integrity of the exam, authors do not have access to the live exam.

Microsoft certifications

Microsoft certifications distinguish you by proving your command of a broad set of skills and experience with current Microsoft products and technologies. The exams and corresponding certifications are developed to validate your mastery of critical competencies as you design and develop or implement and support solutions with Microsoft products and technologies—both on-premises and in the cloud. Certification brings a variety of benefits to the individual and to employers and organizations.

> **MORE INFO   ALL MICROSOFT CERTIFICATIONS**
>
> For information about Microsoft certifications, including a full list of available certifications, go to *microsoft.com/learn*.

Check back often to see what is new!

Errata, updates & book support

We've made every effort to ensure the accuracy of this book and its companion content. You can access updates to this book—in the form of a list of submitted errata and their related corrections—at:

MicrosoftPressStore.com/ERSC9002e/errata

If you discover an error that is not already listed, please submit it to us at the same page.

For additional book support and information, please visit *MicrosoftPressStore.com/Support*.

Please note that product support for Microsoft software and hardware is not offered through the previous addresses. For help with Microsoft software or hardware, go to *support.microsoft.com*.

Stay in touch

Let's keep the conversation going! We're on Twitter: *twitter.com/MicrosoftPress*.

CHAPTER 1

Describe the concepts of security, compliance, and identity

Building a foundational knowledge of key principles applicable to security, compliance, and identity is imperative to any professional who needs to work with Microsoft solutions that target each one of those domains. Some principles will directly correlate with all three domains; some will be more peculiar to each domain. Zero Trust is a great example of a methodology that should extend throughout the entire digital estate of your enterprise and serve as an integrated security philosophy and end-to-end strategy.

Skills covered in this chapter:

- Skill 1.1: Describe security and compliance concepts
- Skill 1.2: Define identity concepts

Skill 1.1: Describe security and compliance concepts

You need to understand common security concepts and terminologies used throughout this book. These concepts will also help build a strong foundational knowledge of security that can be leveraged for other Microsoft security certifications you may plan to take.

This section covers the skills necessary to describe security and compliance concepts according to the Exam SC-900 outline.

> **This skill covers:**
> - Using the shared responsibility model in the cloud
> - Using defense in depth to enhance security by adding multiple layers of protection
> - The guiding principles of Zero Trust methodology
> - Using encryption and hashing to protect data at rest and in transit
> - The concept of governance, what risk means, and the different aspects of compliance

Shared responsibility model

In a traditional datacenter, the IT organization is responsible for the entire infrastructure (except for the networks connecting different physical sites). This is how on-premises computing has worked from the beginning of modern client/server computing (and even before that in the mainframe era). If there was something wrong with the network, storage, or compute infrastructure, the IT organization was responsible for finding out what the problem was and fixing it.

The same went for the security organization. The security organization worked with the IT organization to ensure that all IT infrastructure components were secure. The corporate security organization that set requirements rationalized those requirements with the corporate IT organization, and then defined controls that could be implemented by the IT infrastructure and operations staff. The security organization would also define compliance requirements and be responsible for auditing the infrastructure to make sure that those requirements were met on an ongoing basis.

All this is still true for the on-premises datacenters in your estate. However, with the introduction of public cloud computing, IT and security organizations have a new partner: the cloud service provider (CSP). The CSP has its own IT infrastructure and is responsible for the security requirements and controls implemented on its underlying infrastructures.

This shifts IT to a shared responsibility model for workloads hosted by the CSPs. Which responsibilities are shared varies depending on the exact workload and service, but it roughly aligns with the cloud service model: Infrastructure-as-a-Service (IaaS), Platform-as-a-Service (PaaS), and Software-as-a-Service (SaaS). Figure 1-1 shows how these responsibilities will vary for each service, including on-premises, where the customer has full control over all resources.

As you can see in Figure 1-1, the left column shows 10 core responsibilities that organizations should consider. These responsibilities contribute to achieving a compliant and secure computing environment state. When using cloud computing, physical security is the one responsibility that is wholly owned by cloud service providers (CSP). Physical security is only the full responsibility of the customer in on-premises deployment.

The remaining responsibilities are shared between customers and cloud service providers. Some responsibilities require the CSP and customer to manage and administer the responsibility together. It is important to mention that regardless of the deployment type, the following responsibilities are always retained by the customer: data, endpoints, account, and access management.

Understanding the division of responsibility based on the cloud service delivery model is more than just an academic exercise. When you adopt public cloud services, you'll need to know how to map what you're responsible for and what your cloud service provider is responsible for. Based on this understanding, you'll then define your requirements and adjust your processes, goals, and technical designs.

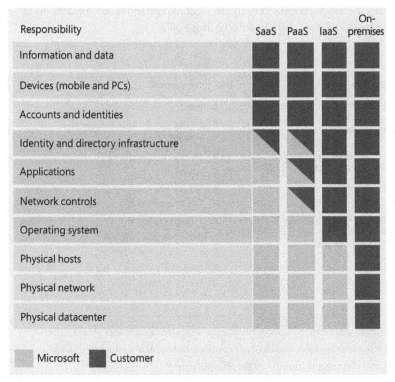

Responsibility	SaaS	PaaS	IaaS	On-premises
Information and data	Customer	Customer	Customer	Customer
Devices (mobile and PCs)	Customer	Customer	Customer	Customer
Accounts and identities	Customer	Customer	Customer	Customer
Identity and directory infrastructure	Microsoft/Customer	Microsoft/Customer	Customer	Customer
Applications	Microsoft	Microsoft/Customer	Customer	Customer
Network controls	Microsoft	Microsoft/Customer	Customer	Customer
Operating system	Microsoft	Microsoft	Customer	Customer
Physical hosts	Microsoft	Microsoft	Microsoft	Customer
Physical network	Microsoft	Microsoft	Microsoft	Customer
Physical datacenter	Microsoft	Microsoft	Microsoft	Customer

Microsoft Customer

FIGURE 1-1 Shared responsibility model

Defense in depth

The principle of defense-in-depth is not new. In fact, it has evolved over the years, though adding multiple layers of protection is the fundamental concept. Doing so makes it hard for the attacker to access the desired data.

This layered approach increases an attacker's risk of detection while reducing an attacker's chance of success. Using this approach, you also enhance your CIA (confidentiality, integrity, and availability, known as the CIA pillars). When you add more layers of protection, you decrease the likelihood that a threat actor will compromise confidential information or alter information that could harm the integrity of the data. Doing so increases the availability level because the threat actor needs to take down multiple layers of protection before they can compromise the overall availability. As you design defense-in-depth layers, it's important to make it harder for attackers to access the desired data (increasing their cost) while ensuring that legitimate users and processes can function well. It is also important to mention that multiple layers of protection can increase the complexity, management, and potential cost. For this reason, it is recommended to use multiple layers of protection that can be managed in a centralized location or at least able to exchange insights with each other to facilitate monitoring and reduce operational costs.

Table 1-1 summarizes the rationale behind each CIA pillar and provides some examples of security controls you can leverage in Azure to enforce those pillars.

TABLE 1-1 CIA pillars

Design principle	Rationale	Security controls
Confidentiality	Ensure that customer's data is accessible only by authorized users/objects	■ Identity Management ■ Isolation ■ Encryption
Integrity	Protect customer's data (compute and storage) against unauthorized changes	■ Identity Management ■ Isolation ■ Encryption ■ Key Management
Availability	Provide numerous levels of redundancy to maximize the availability of customer data	■ Storage replication ■ Geo-redundant storage ■ Disaster recovery process ■ Availability sets ■ Load balancer

> **NOTE** Safety is a critical assurance in operational technology environments where computers control physical machines and processes (such as industrial control systems [ICS] and supervisory control and data acquisition [SCADA] technologies).

Defense-in-depth was a common philosophy when there was a distinct separation of trusted and untrusted networks that were separated by a firewall. Adding multiple layers of protection between the Internet and the internal (trusted) network was commonly discussed and planned (though not always applied consistently in practice). Later, it expanded to include multiple layers of different types of protection per component, as shown in Figure 1-2.

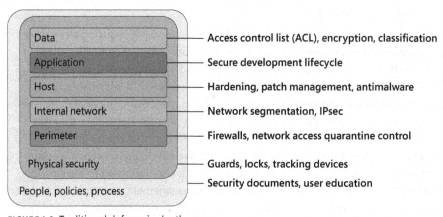

FIGURE 1-2 Traditional defense in depth

The same foundational model applies today but uses different security controls and is easier to apply in a software-defined cloud datacenter like Azure. For example, Azure can provide scale and expertise to protect against large and sophisticated DDoS attacks. However, following our shared responsibility model in cloud computing, customers must also design their applications to be ready for a massive amount of traffic. Some key application capabilities include high availability, scale-out, resiliency, fault tolerance, and attack surface area reduction. Azure DDoS protection is part of the defense-in-depth for Azure Networks approach, as shown in Figure 1-3.

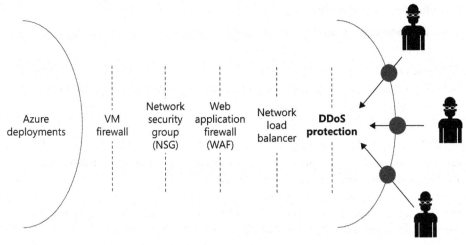

FIGURE 1-3 Azure network defense-in-depth approach

When considering defense-in-depth in an Azure network, you must consider all the security controls around the service you are trying to protect. Also, you need to consider all the other security controls that will be in place between the attacker and the resource that you are trying to protect.

> **MORE INFO   DEFENSE-IN-DEPTH WITH AZURE**
>
> To learn more about the Azure technologies used to provide defense-in-depth, see this overview video at *https://learn.microsoft.com/en-us/shows/azure-videos/ defense-in-depth-security-in-azure.*

Zero Trust Methodology

These days, with users working on different devices from any location and accessing apps across different cloud services, it is critical to keep users' identities secure. The old security assumption that everything on the corporate network behind the firewall is considered to be trusted is no longer correct. With cloud adoption, identity becomes the new perimeter, the preferred control plane for your entire infrastructure, regardless of the location on-premises or in the cloud. You use the user's identity to control access to any services from any device and obtain visibility and insights into how your data is being used.

Zero Trust describes an approach to security and a mindset that shifts security defenses from static, network-based perimeters to dynamic protections focused on users, assets, and resources. Also, as the name implies, you start by not trusting anything and always verifying trustworthiness explicitly. The guiding principles of the Zero Trust methodology are as follows:

- **Always verify**   Make sure that you always authenticate and authorize access based on all available elements, which can include a user's identity, location, device health, data classification, service, or workload.

- **Use least privilege access**   Whenever possible, use just-in-time (JIT) and just-enough-access (JEA) to ensure better data protection.

- **Assume breach**   If you always assume that an attacker has gained some access to the environment, you can create better security controls for each system component. This principle enables you to both prevent incidents and rapidly respond to them.

EXAM TIP

Make sure you remember those guiding principles because there is a high probability that you will be questioned about them on the SC-900 exam.

Microsoft suggests the implementation of Zero Trust controls and technologies across six foundational elements, represented in Figure 1-4.

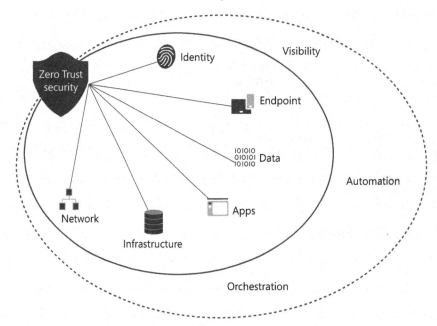

FIGURE 1-4 Zero Trust across the enterprise

Each one of those elements will have general design considerations that should be addressed, as well as unique requirements from the organization's perspective. At the same time, each element has its core security best practices that should be applied. The following list provides more details about these elements:

- **Identity**   When an identity attempts to access a resource, it is important to ensure the risk is low that an attacker is controlling the account. The identity risk level of a session can vary by the strength of the authentication and how similar the attributes and signals are to the normal expected behavior of the account.

- **Endpoint**   Make sure you monitor and enforce device health and compliance before granting resource access to users on that device.

- **Data**   Data is the primary storage value that must be protected, which means the security system must understand its value (using classification labels) and apply the proper security policies, which apply the proper level of security where they go.

- **Apps**   Apps allow people and systems to access data, and they generate business value that must be protected. You need to apply controls and technologies to

  - Discover all your apps (including shadow IT)

  - Set the right access policies

  - Ensure that the appropriate controls and configurations are applied to the apps (including the access model)

  - Allow or deny access based on real-time data and analytics; monitor for any abnormal behavior

  - Make sure that you rapidly respond to attacks on the apps to limit the time that attackers have access to them

- **Infrastructure**   Regardless of your infrastructure location (on-premises, in the cloud, or hybrid), make sure that you have good security hygiene (security patches, secure configurations, and so on) and that you detect attacks and anomalies using all available telemetry. Automatically block and flag risky behavior and take protective actions.

- **Network**   The network provides connectivity and access control, so it should be closely aligned to an overall enterprise access-control strategy that also includes identity controls. Providing private networks for existing applications that protect against unsolicited Internet traffic network (such as network segmentation) is still a good practice. However, you can also apply more granular micro-segmentation to further protect workloads from attacks on the private network. Migrating workloads to the cloud is the ideal moment to improve your real-time threat protection, end-to-end encryption, monitoring, and analytics across all networks.

Microsoft's vision of Zero Trust also includes full visibility across all those elements in an integrated interface. With each area generating its own relevant alerts, we need an integrated capability to manage the resulting influx of data to better defend against threats and validate trust in a transaction. It is also important to wrap up integrating those elements with automation and orchestration to facilitate both the implementation and the response time for incidents.

You need governance to give you more visibility and policy management to ensure everything is in place. Zero Trust allows you to automate the enforcement of security policies, ensuring compliant access decisions and configurations throughout the enterprise. The access policies should be used to consistently decide whether to allow access, deny access, or dynamically manage risk in real time by asking for additional authentication challenges (such as multifactor authentication) or applying access restrictions to the session. Figure 1-5 shows an example of how this high-level architecture looks.

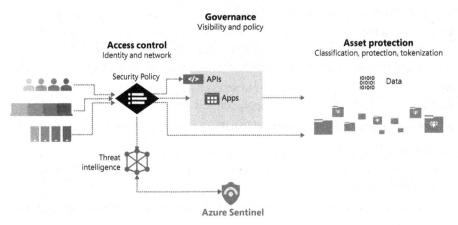

FIGURE 1-5 Zero Trust implementation

Notice in Figure 1-5 that the security policy enables users and devices to have a seamless and secure experience when accessing data directly or from an application. It is also important to call out the visibility of security operations using Microsoft Sentinel as a Security Information and Event Management (SIEM) system to consolidate all events and alerts triggered across different services. Using a modern SIEM platform such as Microsoft Sentinel is imperative for Zero Trust because the SIEM relies heavily on signal and solution integration to succeed.

It is also very important to understand that not every organization has the same maturity level to implement Zero Trust across all segments and use the latest and greatest technologies. When you evaluate a scenario, you need to consider the organization's maturity level when planning which steps to take first. Let's use the following companies as an example:

- Contoso's current scenario:
  - On-premises identity with a partial level of single-sign-on (SSO).
  - IT has limited visibility across the different workloads and the device's health status.
  - Flat network infrastructure.
- Fabrikam's current scenario:
  - Hybrid identity (integrated cloud and on-premises identities).
  - Policies in place to grant access to data, apps, and network.

- Segmented networks.
- Fabrikam has started utilizing analytics to better understand users' behavior and identify threats.

These two organizations are at different stages of their journeys. Contoso has basic, traditional capabilities that are heavily dependent on on-premises resources. Fabrikam has more advanced maturity and has already started using a modern hybrid identity and analytics.

When planning the implementation of Zero Trust for both organizations, you will see that you need to start with what they have and move forward with that. A reasonable goal is to move Contoso to be more like Fabrikam. Fabrikam's goal should be set to a more optimal maturity model, such as implementing passwordless authentication and determining risk with real-time behavior analyses.

> **MORE INFO**   **IMPLEMENTATION DETAILS BY SEGMENT**
>
> The SC-900 exam doesn't go into implementation details for each of those segments, but you can use the following resources to learn more about them:
>
> - **Identity**   *http://aka.ms/ZTIdentity*
> - **Endpoints**   *http://aka.ms/ZTEndpoints*
> - **Applications**   *http://aka.ms/ZTApplications*
> - **Data**   *http://aka.ms/ZTData*
> - **Infrastructure**   *http://aka.ms/ZTInfrastructure*
> - **Networks**   *http://aka.ms/ZTNetwork*

Encryption and hashing

When migrating to the cloud, you should make sure that the data is protected no matter where this data is located. Data is stored and transferred over multiple systems, so you need to think about the different locations of the data over time.

Figure 1-6 illustrates the following five stages:

1. **Data at rest in the user's device**   In this stage, the data is located at the endpoint, which can be any device. You should always enforce data encryption at rest for company- and user-owned devices (bring your own device [BYOD]).

2. **Data in transit from the user's device to the cloud**   When data leaves the user's device, you should ensure that the data is still protected. Many technologies (for example, Azure AD Information Protection) can encrypt the data regardless of location. It is also imperative to ensure that the transport channel is encrypted, therefore enforcing the use of the transport layer security (TLS) to transfer the data.

3. **Data at rest in the cloud provider's datacenter**   When the data arrives in the cloud provider's servers, their storage infrastructure should ensure redundancy and protection. Make sure you understand how your CSP performs data encryption at rest, who is responsible for managing the keys, and how data redundancy is performed.

4. **Data in transit from the cloud to on-premises**   In this case, the same recommendations specified in stage two (data in transit from the user's device to the cloud) are applicable. Enforce data encryption on the file itself and encrypt the transport layer.

5. **Data at rest on-premises**   Customers are responsible for keeping their data secure on-premises. Data encryption at rest at the organization's datacenter is a critical step to accomplish that. Make sure you have the correct infrastructure to enable encryption, data redundancy, and key management.

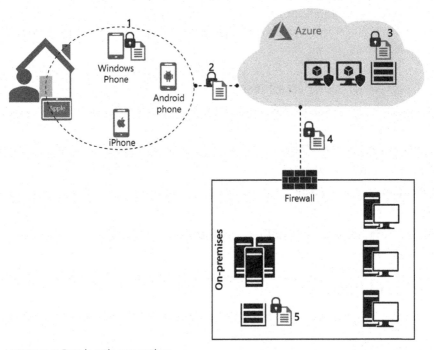

FIGURE 1-6 Data locations over time

While encryption is important, it is also critical to protect the keys used to encrypt and decrypt them (which may be managed by you or the cloud provider).

You should also consider other security controls to enhance the confidentiality and integrity of the information. You can digitally sign the message that you want to transmit. Based on that digital signature, the user can verify that the data has not been changed since it was signed. Another advantage of using this method is that the identity of the user who signed the data can also be verified.

To enhance the integrity of the text that will be transmitted, you can also apply a hash of the text (also called a *digest*). The receiver can then compute a hash on the data received and compare the computed hash with the received hash. If it matches, the received data has not been altered.

MORE INFO   **DIGITAL SIGNATURES**

For more detailed information about digital signatures, see https://learn.microsoft.com/
en-us/windows/win32/seccrypto/digital-signatures.

Governance, risk, and compliance (GRC)

Governance can be defined as the system of rules, practices, and processes used by an organization to direct and control its activities. External standards, obligations, and expectations can dictate governance activities. But governance goes beyond that; it can also help organizations achieve objectives and incorporate most management areas, including internal controls, performance measurement, and corporate disclosure.

Risk management is the process of identifying, assessing, and responding to threats or events that can impact the organization's objectives. Often, governance is applied via security controls to reduce or remediate risk.

When you hear people say, "My company needs to be compliant with," it usually means that this company needs to adhere to country/region, state or federal laws, or even multi-national regulations. These regulations define what types of data must be protected, what processes are required under the legislation, and what penalties are issued to organizations that fail to comply. When organizations need to meet compliance requirements in highly regulated industries like government, finance, and healthcare, they need to certify their workload's configurations in the cloud or on-premises can meet the security specifications defined in a specific framework, such as CIS, NIST, or PCI.

When talking about compliance, you also need to consider regulations regarding *data residency*, in other words, where the data resides physically. You also need to consider *data sovereignty*, which is the principle that data, particularly personal data, is subject to the laws and regulations of the country/region in which it's physically collected, held, or processed. Finally, you also need to consider data privacy, which also varies according to laws and regulations.

Using the Microsoft Defender for Cloud regulatory compliance dashboard, you can monitor your compliance status in a multicloud environment. Defender for Cloud provides security recommendations that map to different industry compliance standards.

When an organization must comply with a certain standard based on the operating industry, it is important to identify the workloads deployed across multiple cloud providers and have the security posture visibility in a single dashboard. For example, if the organization is part of the financial industry, it might need to comply with the Payment Card Industry (PCI) Data Security Standard (DSS) standard. When you need to monitor your multicloud workloads based on an industry standard, you can also leverage the same regulatory compliance dashboard in Defender for Cloud.

EXAM TIP

GRC aims to enable organizations to reduce risk and improve compliance effectiveness by implementing a compliance and risk management framework.

Skill 1.2: Define identity concepts

Organizations planning to adopt cloud computing must be aware of the identity and access management methods available and of how these methods will integrate with their current on-premises infrastructures. These days, with users working on different devices from any location and accessing apps across different cloud services, it is critical to keep the user's identity secure. Indeed, with cloud adoption, identity becomes the new perimeter, the control panel for your entire infrastructure, regardless of the location, whether on-premises or in the cloud.

You use the user's identity to control access to any services from any device and to obtain visibility and insights into how your data is being used. This section covers the identity concept skills according to the Exam SC-900 outline.

This skill covers:

- Aspects of identity used as the primary security perimeter
- How authentication works and the difference between authentication and authorization
- Using federation services and identity providers
- Using directory services to authenticate users

Define identity as the primary security perimeter

Modern environments are going through another radical change. Previously, our work environment mostly existed on local intranets. Employees used their corporate computers from within the corporate offices to access company resources such as file servers. The firewall was the perimeter boundary for the network. Anything inside the firewall was a company resource and was considered safe. Anything outside was the Internet and could be malicious.

Some users did portions of their jobs remotely by taking their corporate machines home with them. To access the corporate network, we added VPNs into the mix. Again, our firewalls were still the security perimeters for our environment.

Eventually, we saw the rise in cloud-based applications that lived solely on the Internet. At first, many companies still require users to access these resources from the corporate network, either physically in the corporate office or remotely through a VPN.

This strategy had drawbacks. First, network performance is not always ideal. It is slow and costly to use a high-speed Internet connection to send traffic back to the corporate network and then immediately send it back to the Internet to the cloud resource and back the same way to the user. Second, users started using non-corporate, personally owned devices like mobile phones and tablets. Requiring them to use VPN to access the corporate network was not acceptable.

Today, corporations have users who work from the corporate office, at home, or in reality, anywhere. They access resources on the corporate network or fully on the Internet. And they are doing all this from company-owned devices and personally owned computers and mobile devices. The traditional security perimeter is still useful but not enough to protect a modern-day company.

Identity is the only consistent thing across all these different combinations of scenarios in this modern environment, so it must be the new security perimeter for enterprises. This is a difficult shift in thinking for some companies to make, but it is clearly needed. With identity as the security perimeter point of view, we need to increase our security in the identity space. As you'll see later in this chapter, Azure Active Directory's conditional access will let us enforce policy to ensure security conditions are met before we allow access to resources. We also have several ways to strengthen our identity credentials with passwordless-based authentication and other forms of multifactor authentication (MFA) using Windows Hello for Business or an authenticator app. This is extremely important because identity is the starting point for many attacks.

Authentication

From a conceptual standpoint, authentication, sometimes abbreviated as *AuthN*, is simply the act of something or someone proving its identity to something else. In other words, a person or device proves they are who or what they claim to be. You come across authentication many times in your daily life. You have just authenticated when you log in to your computer with your username and password. When you log in to check your email through a browser or an application like Outlook, you have authenticated with your email provider.

When you pick up your mobile device and use a biometric such as a fingerprint or your face to unlock the device, you have completed authentication again. If you go to the ATM to withdraw money, you must first provide a card and a PIN. If you successfully authenticate, you can then withdraw money from your account (if you have funds). You usually complete authentication dozens of times a day and don't even think about it.

There are many different authentication factors; we'll cover some of those in more depth later in this chapter. These authentication factors can be something you know, something you have, or something you are. The most common factors are username and password. However, these are the most easily compromised by an attacker. Multifactor authentication is also growing in popularity (although slower than it should), where multiple authentication method types are required to authenticate — the username and password and another form of authentication. Text messages or phone calls are the most common forms of multifactor authentication, but there are also methods such as a one-time passcode (OTP), where the passcode can be used only once and is usually good for a limited time. Authenticator apps, such as the Microsoft Authenticator app, send a push notification to the device that the user approves.

As previously mentioned, biometrics such as fingerprints and facial recognition are commonly used. Non-human identities need to be authenticated, too. Computers and services authenticate using certificates, shared secrets (just a password for an application), or specific protocols such as Kerberos. Authentication is not just for people! Figure 1-7 shows some of these common authentication methods.

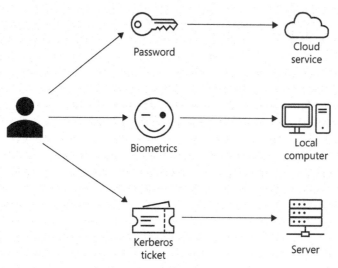

FIGURE 1-7 Common authentication methods

Figure 1-7 is not meant to show an exhaustive list of authentication methods; instead, it shows that there are many ways for someone or something to prove that it is who or what it claims to be. This can be human-to-service authentication or service-to-service authentication. Everything starts with authentication.

Authorization

Authorization is another critical part of identity and access management. Authorization is sometimes abbreviated as *AuthZ*. Conceptually, you can think of authorization as what something is allowed to do. Once the system or services knows who you are — authentication — you have rights or permissions to do things — authorization. These rights can be as simple as viewing a file (a *grant* permission) or denying the ability to view a file (a *deny* permission).

You've probably experienced this when someone sends you a file or a link to a site, and when you try to open the file or visit the site, you receive an Access Denied error message. This means you don't have the authorization to access that resource. You experience authorization when you *can*, or you are allowed to view a file or access a site. The difference is that you don't get a message saying you are allowed to view it! You probably come across hundreds, if not thousands, of authorization decisions a day and don't even realize it (unless you get denied, of course).

Authorization decisions can be made based on many factors. If you have a specific role assigned to your account, you might have inherited permissions in the system to add, modify, delete, or view things. This is commonly referred to as Role-Based Access Control (RBAC). For example, if you hold the Global Administrator role in Azure Active Directory, you can manage all aspects of Azure Active Directory. The Global Reader role can view all the same things as the Global Administrator role; Global Readers just can't make any changes.

Authorization decisions might also be made based on information about the user. For example, if you are a member of a sales organization, you would probably be a member of an Active Directory sales group. This group membership would grant you access to the sales department's shared network folder or a SharePoint site, but you wouldn't be able to access the engineering department's shared network folder or SharePoint site. Only those who are members of the engineering group would be able to access these resources. Typically, these decisions are made by Access Control Lists (ACLs) determined by the system administrator.

Another example of authorization based on information about the user could be their title. When a regular user logs into their HR application, they see information about themselves, such as how many hours they've worked and their manager, pay stub, and information about their benefits. They are only authorized to view their information. Their manager has a similar view but probably also has additional information they can see about their employees. They can see all the hours worked for their direct reports but can't see the same information about other employees in the organization. Managers can only see additional information about their direct reports based on their titles. Finally, the head of HR might see a wide range of information about the company, such as the total hours worked for everyone in the company, total payroll, and benefits spent. Because they hold a high-ranking position, they are authorized to see all this information. Most authorization is done at the application level using this RBAC model.

Authorization applies to non-human accounts as well. A service account can hold roles in Azure Active Directory, which would have the same permissions as any human account with that role. Service accounts can also be members of groups. A common example of this is the service that runs the backups. Depending on the design, it might require membership to a high-privilege group, such as **Backup Operators**, to back up and restore files on the system.

Hopefully, the concept of authorization is clear and straightforward for you. Authorization grants or denies permissions to various resources for both human and non-human accounts. However, the implementation details of this can be extremely complex. The sales and engineering teams can access separate corporate resources in the above example.

However, what do these teams do when collaborating on something? For example, let's say that the engineering team has a new product coming out, and the sales team needs to be able to sell it. Following are some things you will need to consider:

- Do we add the sales team to the engineering group?
- Should we add the engineering team to the sales group?
- Or do we create a new sales-engineering group and add the sales and engineering groups to that new group?

This last option might seem like the right answer, but what do we do when the operations group also needs to work with engineering to ensure the production of the product meets engineering standards? Operations also needs to work with sales to make sure the supply chain is aligned with their sales projections. Do we create more groups for all three teams to work together? As you can see, this starts to grow and get out of hand. Having an authorization design for these types of scenarios is important before you start implementing an identity access management (IAM) solution. This type of scenario is pretty normal, and some of these decisions can be made ahead of time, but you will also need to plan for how you will handle exception cases and new scenarios that will arise. You will need that flexibility as business needs and scenarios grow.

Lastly, we also need to ensure we follow the least-privilege concept regarding authorization. Human and non-human accounts should only have the minimum authorization permissions required to accomplish their tasks. It is easy to grant more permissions, and things will work if we do that, but we'll pay the price later for those decisions, often in catastrophic ways. It's also often much more difficult to remove permissions from users and non-human accounts after they work. There is a fear that something might break or that someone will not be able to do their job, either of which would impact the business. From the start, you should take the time to ensure the least privilege is being followed for authorization decisions. Your future self will thank you.

> **MORE INFO**   **AZURE AD ROLES AND LEAST-PRIVILEGE ROLES**
>
> You can learn more about Azure AD Roles and what they are authorized to do at *https://aka.ms/SC900_AADRoles* and *https://aka.ms/SC900_TaskByLeastPrivilege*.

Federation and identity providers

Before we get into the components of federation services, it's important to first understand why we need them. For example, let's say that an application doesn't reside on a corporate intranet, so we need a way to leverage existing authentication methods. The easiest way to solve this dilemma is to create a username and password for that application, though doing so has some problems. The first problem is that each application must implement its own authentication stack and everything that comes with it, such as password resets and storage of these credentials. There are numerous cases where a vendor does not correctly store these usernames and passwords, and they are compromised.

To make matters worse, users will likely reuse their credentials across multiple applications, including sharing credentials between work and home. Credential reuse presents an even bigger issue as the number of SaaS applications increases because the credentials are spread across all these applications. A compromise of one credential can lead to a compromise of all the remaining applications.

The next issue is that applications typically need more than just a username to be useful to a user. Data points such as a user's job title, department, manager, and so on are leveraged in applications to allow functionality and provide authorization for user actions. As discussed previously, what a department head can view, add, delete, and change is much different from what an individual employee can do in that application. This additional data would also need to be present in each SaaS application.

Federation services solve these issues. A detailed breakdown of the inner workings of federation protocols such as WS-Fed, SAML, OAuth, and OpenID Connect is well beyond the scope of this book. However, some components and concepts worth understanding apply to many modern authentication protocols.

> **MORE INFO   FEDERATION SERVICES**
>
> You can learn more about Federation Services at *https://learn.microsoft.com/en-us/windows-server/identity/ad-fs/deployment/how-to-connect-fed-azure-adfs*.

The identity provider, frequently abbreviated as IdP, handles the user's authentication. The authentication can be via a web browser using forms-based authentication, integrated Windows authentication (IWA), or a web API application. IdP is really user authentication as a service. Common examples of IdPs are Azure AD, Active Directory Federation Services (ADFS), and Ping Federate. The IdP will then issue claims to the application, also frequently called a resource provider that trusts the IdP. The user is then signed into the application.

Claims are information that is sent to the application/resource provider that, in this case, identifies the user and any additional information about the user that the application needs to function. The necessary information varies from application to application, but information such as title, manager, employee ID, and the like can be included in the claim. This claim is signed by the IdP using the IdP's private key.

Public key cryptography is used by the IdP to digitally sign claims using its private key. The application/resource provider uses the public key to validate the claim. The application validates that the claim came from the IdP, assuming the private key has not been compromised and that the claims data has not been modified since it was signed.

A federation trust must first be set up before a user can authenticate, have information sent as a claim to the application, and access that information. The setup details vary between federation protocols, but the IdP and the application will essentially exchange some information, such as the IdP public key and the application's endpoints for authentication. Typically, this is in the trust's metadata.

The application or resource provider is what the user is accessing. Because the trust and metadata exchange have happened previously, the application will trust the signed claims from the IdP. Thousands of applications, such as Office365, ServiceNow, and WorkDay, support this federated authentication model. We can see all these pieces together in Figure 1-8, which shows an identity provider sending a signed claim to an application/resource provider. A two-way arrow connects the identity provider to the application/resource provider to indicate a trust and that metadata is being exchanged.

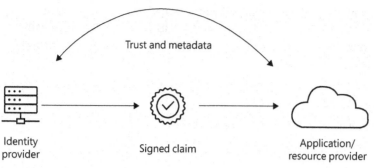

FIGURE 1-8 Federation components working together.

Active Directory

Windows Server Active Directory is a multi-master, on-premises directory service that's been built into the Windows operating system since Windows 2000. Typically, it is the primary on-premises identity directory for an enterprise and is widely used (it's used by 95 percent of Fortune 500 companies). If you have seen the *Ctrl+Alt+Delete* screen at your corporate workstation, entered your corporate username and password, and successfully logged in with a work account, you've used Active Directory. Numerous books have been written about Active Directory, and we can't go into that depth about it here, though it is still important to understand the basics because we will build on them later in this chapter.

Active Directory provides authentication, authorization, and usually a single sign-on experience to corporate resources such as file servers, email, and other local intranet applications. Active Directory will have accounts for users and computers, as well as accounts for applications and services. Groups and printers will also be stored in Active Directory. Active Directory supports many protocols like LDAP, NTLM, Kerberos, and DNS. It also can apply security policies to computers and users through group policy. From an administrative perspective, all these objects can be managed hierarchically in containers and organizational units (OUs), as shown in Figure 1-9.

The boundary for Active Directory is the Active Directory Forest. Everything in this forest trusts one another inherently. This boundary can be extended to other Active Directory forests as well. Typically, boundaries are used in merger and acquisition scenarios and some older architectures with separate resource forests for applications.

Though still extremely popular, Active Directory is very much a product of the late 1990s and early 2000s. It was designed for a different world from what exists today. It was assumed that the resources you accessed were on the local intranet and that you would be physically in the office. If people had Internet access at home, it was through slow, dial-up connections. Very few people had "dumb" cell phones, and some had pagers. Cloud-backed resources such as SaaS applications and the protocols they leverage (for example, WS-Fed, SAML, OAuth, and OpenIDConnect) hadn't been created yet.

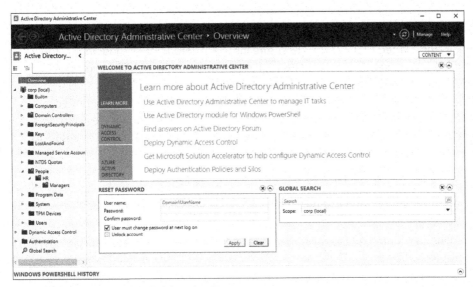

FIGURE 1-9 Active Directory Administrative Center

Once resources began leaving their intranets for the Internet, Active Directory began to face some challenges, chiefly providing secure access to these modern resources from their corporate accounts for corporate users. Enter the need for federation services.

> **MORE INFO**   **ACTIVE DIRECTORY COMPARED TO AZURE ACTIVE DIRECTORY**
>
> You can see how Active Directory features compare to Azure Active Directory's features at *https://aka.ms/SC900_ADCompareToAAD.*

Thought experiment

In this thought experiment, demonstrate your skills and knowledge of the topics covered in this chapter. You can find answers to this thought experiment in the next section.

> **Thought experiment**
>
> **Contoso's Journey to the Cloud**
>
> You are one of the IT administrators for Contoso, an online general store specializing in various products for use around the home. Contoso is starting its journey to the cloud, and you need to evaluate different cloud providers to understand their privacy principles and compliance resources. It is very important to them that this cloud provider takes privacy seriously and doesn't use their information for advertising purposes.

You are going to lead the creation of a new team at Contoso called Cloud Security, and one of the charters of this team is to ensure the use of Zero Trust methodology across all available segments. Contoso plans to start its journey to the cloud by implementing more IaaS resources while keeping some workloads on-premises. The only PaaS service they plan to use is the identity provider, which they want to ensure is synchronized with their on-premises Active Directory. Contoso also wants to monitor the compliance status of their workloads from a single pane of glass. Lastly, Contoso wants to ensure its customer data is accessible only by authorized users/objects.

With this information in mind, answer the following questions:

1. Who is responsible for maintaining the operating system updates on VMs in an IaaS scenario?

2. What can Contoso use to see the compliance status of their cloud and on-premises workload?

3. What Zero Trust guiding principle ensures you always authenticate and authorize access based on all available elements?

4. What design principle must Contoso use to ensure its customer data is accessible only by authorized users/objects?

Thought experiment answers

This section contains the solution to the thought experiment.

1. In an IaaS scenario, the customer is responsible for updating the operating system running on the VMs.

2. Microsoft Defender for Cloud.

3. Always verify.

4. Confidentiality.

Chapter summary

- Cloud providers adopt the shared responsibility model that adjusts itself according to the cloud service model: infrastructure as a service (IaaS), platform as a service (PaaS), and software as a service (SaaS).

- Defense in depth increases an attacker's risk of detection while reducing an attacker's chance of success.

- Zero Trust guiding principles are: always verify, user least privilege access, and assume breach.

- Zero Trust should be applied across the following segments: Identity, Endpoint, Data, Apps, Infrastructure, and Network.

- Regardless of the deployment type, the customer always retains the following responsibilities: data, endpoints, account, and access management.

- While encryption is becoming imperative, you should also consider other security controls to enhance the confidentiality and integrity of the information. You can digitally sign the message you want to transmit, and based on that digital signature, the user can verify that the data has not been changed since it was signed.

- When organizations need to meet compliance requirements in highly regulated industries like government, finance, and healthcare, they need to certify their workload's configurations in the cloud or on-premises can meet the security specifications defined in a specific framework, such as CIS, NIST, or PCI.

- Authentication, sometimes abbreviated as AuthN, is simply the act of something or someone proving its identity to something else. In other words, a person or device proves they are who or what they claim to be.

- Conceptually, you can think of authorization as what something is allowed to do. Once the system or services knows who you are — authentication — you have rights or permissions to do things — authorization.

- Federation services enable the access of services across organizational or domain boundaries by establishing trust relationships between the respective domain's identity providers.

- Active Directory is a set of directory services developed by Microsoft as part of Windows 2000 for on-premises domain-based networks.

CHAPTER 2

Microsoft identity and access management solutions

Identity and access management is a core foundational piece for security and compliance. Everything today starts with identity. Users have identities to access resources such as applications, and they can do that from anywhere on the planet. Applications themselves have identities to define their permission scopes. Computer objects have identities and can be used as a factor to make access decisions. Understanding identity concepts and capabilities is a requirement for properly achieving security and compliance in your organization.

Skills in this chapter:

- Skill 2.1: Define the function and identity types of Microsoft Entra ID
- Skill 2.2: Describe the authentication capabilities of Microsoft Entra ID
- Skill 2.3: Describe access management capabilities of Microsoft Entra ID
- Skill 2.4: Describe the identity protection and governance capabilities of Microsoft Entra

Skill 2.1: Define the function and identity types of Microsoft Entra ID

This objective deals with the fundamental concepts of Microsoft Entra ID. In this section, you'll learn what Microsoft Entra ID is and its key enterprise features. You'll also learn about internal and external identities, hybrid identity, and the different ways to authenticate to Microsoft Entra ID.

> **This skill covers:**
> - Microsoft Entra for unified identity and network access
> - Microsoft Entra's key features
> - Hybrid identity setups
> - Microsoft Entra identities, including users, devices, groups, and workloads

Describe what Microsoft Entra is

Microsoft Entra is a product suite focusing on unified identity and network access for businesses. This new suite was announced in May 2022 and consists of the following identity and network components across three key areas:

Identity and access management

- Microsoft Entra ID is formerly known as Azure Active Directory and is the key focus of this chapter. This core IAM (Identity and Access Management) product allows you to manage and protect users, apps, workload identities, and devices.
- Microsoft Entra ID Governance is discussed in Skill 2.4 and allows businesses to automatically ensure that the right people have the right access to the right apps and services at the right time.
- Microsoft Entra External ID provides functionality to allow business partners and customers secure access to resources and applications.

New identity categories

- Microsoft Entra Verified ID issues and verifies credentials based on open standards to quickly onboard employees, partners, and customers and uses the credentials anywhere that supports those open standards.
- Microsoft Entra Permissions Management is discussed in Skill 2.4 and allows you to manage your identity permissions across your multicloud (Azure, AWS, and GCP) infrastructure.
- Microsoft Entra Workload ID helps apps and services (nonhuman identities) securely access cloud resources.

Network access

- Microsoft Entra Internet Access allows secure access to the Internet and Software as a Service (SaaS) and Microsoft 365 applications.
- Microsoft Entra Private Access allows a secure connection to private apps that would usually require a VPN or other legacy protocols like NTLM or Kerberos to access them.

Describe what Microsoft Entra ID is

Microsoft Entra ID is Microsoft's cloud-based Identity-as-a-Service (IDaaS) offering. It is an IAM product with 400 million monthly active users and tens of billions of authentications processed daily! Many of the IAM features are covered throughout this chapter, but let's take a high-level view of some of the key features to help give you an idea of what makes up Microsoft Entra ID.

Applications

Microsoft Entra ID is the Identity Provider (IdP) for Microsoft applications such as Office365 and Azure. It also leverages modern protocols such as WS-Federation, SAML, OAuth, and OpenID Connect to integrate with non-Microsoft applications. The Microsoft Entra Application Gallery has thousands of pre-integrated applications, making authentication to these apps easy to set up. Also, the Application Gallery uses the SCIM (System for Cross-domain Identity Management) protocol for provisioning users to and de-provisioning users from these applications. If the application is not in the gallery, you can still integrate it with Microsoft Entra ID yourself, or you can request that it should be added to the gallery. You can also build your own applications that call the Microsoft Graph or other Microsoft APIs, your own APIs, and get tokens. The Microsoft Authentication Library (MSAL) is available to help accelerate your developer teams with these tasks.

Application proxy

Application proxy is used to provide remote access to on-premises web applications. This allows any conditional access policies to apply when accessing these on-premises applications without making any changes to the application itself. This is an excellent way to leverage your cloud-based identity security to protect your existing on-premises applications. All connectivity is outbound to Microsoft Entra ID. These applications will appear to the user as any other application. There is no difference to the user if the application is on-premises or in the cloud. They access it in the same way.

Authentication

Skill 2.2 is focused on the authentication aspects of Microsoft Entra ID, such as password hash sync (PHS), pass-through authentication (PTA), federation, multifactor authentication (MFA), passwordless methods such as Windows Hello for Business, Certificate-based, FIDO2, and Microsoft Entra Password Protection.

Access management

Skill 2.3 is focused on the access management aspects of Microsoft Entra ID, specifically the conditional access feature. At a high level, you can define which users or groups must meet a specific criterion, such as completing MFA or having a specific device or platform type, before they can access a resource, such as a specific application or the applications in your tenant. Many different Microsoft Entra roles can be assigned to administrators to follow the principle of least-privilege while also granting them the necessary access to perform necessary tasks. You will also see the concept of least-privilege later in Microsoft Entra Permissions Management.

Devices

Microsoft Intune is the primary device management platform for cloud-based devices, but there are device objects in Microsoft Entra ID that are Microsoft Entra–registered, Microsoft Entra hybrid–joined, or Microsoft Entra–joined. We'll cover Microsoft Entra hybrid–joined devices in more detail in the next section, but these devices can be used as a control in conditional access that must be met before accessing the resource. Just be aware that devices do exist in Microsoft Entra ID, but the traditional management you think of with group policy Objects (GPOs) is performed from Microsoft Intune. However, there is a tight relationship between Microsoft Entra ID and Microsoft Intune.

Domain services

Microsoft Entra Domain Services lets you join your Azure virtual machines to a traditional Active Directory domain. This is separate from your on-premises Active Directory domain but is populated from your Microsoft Entra tenant. You can think of this as a resource forest for legacy protocols like NTLM, Kerberos, and LDAP for applications that have been lifted and shifted into Azure.

External identities

Microsoft Entra enables easy collaboration with other companies using Microsoft Entra Business-to-Business (B2B) that share resources like documents or access applications. You would use Azure AD Business-to-Consumer (B2C) if you are creating customer-facing apps that are fully featured Customer Identity and Access Management (CIAM) solutions. Azure Active Directory B2C is a totally separate Microsoft Entra tenant. Both Microsoft Entra B2B and Azure AD B2C support conditional access.

Governance

Skill 2.4 is focused on the governance aspects of Microsoft Entra ID. These features include Lifecycle Workflows, Access Reviews, and several aspects of Entitlement Management, from automatic assignment and using Microsoft Entra Verified ID to improve onboarding. The primary focus of governance is determining which users should access which resources. The governance process must also be auditable to verify that it is working.

Reporting

Various log sources are available, from directory changes in audit logs to sign-in logs for interactive and noninteractive events. Microsoft Entra also includes logs for applications and managed-service identities—a specific type of application identity. You can also see Microsoft Graph API activity from these apps, such as if the application is enumerating the directory or the privileges these applications use. These can all be accessed in the Microsoft Entra portal or exported to Log Analytics, Microsoft Sentinel, or any other SIEM.

EXAM TIP

Remember the different features used for Microsoft Entra ID and which problems they solve for a company.

Licensing

Microsoft Entra ID has four core levels of licensing:

- **Microsoft Entra ID Free**   Microsoft Entra ID Free provides user and group management and directory sync. This is included when you sign up for Office 365 or Microsoft 365 resources.

- **Microsoft Entra ID P1**   This level includes most of the features discussed in this chapter. This includes conditional access, self-service password reset with writeback, dynamic groups, and much more.

- **Microsoft Entra ID P2**   This level includes some governance capabilities, such as basic access reviews, basic entitlement management, and privilege identity management. It also includes identity protection and advanced security features.

- **Microsoft Entra ID Governance**   This level includes advanced governance capabilities that can be extended onto the existing governance capabilities in P1 or P2, such as using entitlement management with customer extensions (Logic Apps) or Lifecycle Workflows (LCW).

MORE INFO   MICROFT ENTRA ID FEATURES BY LICENSE

For a detailed breakdown of what features are included in each license level, see https://aka.ms/SC900_ME-IDLicensing.

EXAM TIP

Remember which features are part of Microsoft Entra ID P2 and Microsoft Entra ID Governance. The rest are included in Microsoft Entra ID P1.

Describe what hybrid identity is

Very few customers are starting with a completely greenfield environment (a from-scratch and totally new environment) with only Microsoft Entra ID accounts accessing only cloud resources. Most customers are in a hybrid identity state with their Microsoft Entra tenant(s) connected to an on-premises AD. This is where user accounts must exist in the on-premises Active Directory and in Microsoft Entra ID. The user might access a local file server and then access their email in Office365. They need to be able to do this with one seamless account. Hybrid identity makes this possible. You must use a hybrid identity to leverage your existing Active Directory environment and take advantage of Microsoft Entra ID.

There are two distinct components to a hybrid identity setup:

- Syncing of the users and their attributes from Active Directory to Microsoft Entra ID.
- Authenticating to Microsoft Entra ID using credentials from on-premises Active Directory. This can be accomplished via password hash sync (PHS), pass-through authentication (PTA), or federation.

Microsoft Entra Connect

Microsoft Entra Connect is one of the tools used to create users, groups, and other objects in Microsoft Entra ID. The information is sourced from your on-premises Active Directory, which is the usual scenario for most customers using a hybrid identity. Changes in your on-premises directory to those objects are automatically synced to Microsoft Entra ID. The source of authority (SOA) for these objects is the on-premises Active Directory, meaning the sync is one-way from Active Directory to Microsoft Entra ID.

Microsoft Entra Connect has a very robust setup wizard to help you with this process. You use the express setup to choose the default options for you, or you can do a custom installation to get extremely granular with your choices. You can select which objects will be synced to Microsoft Entra ID (and which attributes of those objects, if needed).

Another part of the setup wizard helps you pick which authentication method your users will use to authenticate to Microsoft Entra ID, as shown in Figure 2-1.

Microsoft Entra Connect is a key piece of hybrid infrastructure and must be protected like you would protect a domain controller in Active Directory. If an attacker were to access a Microsoft Entra Connect server, this would be the security equivalent of getting access to a domain controller.

> **MORE INFO MICROSOFT ENTRA CONNECT**
>
> You can read more about customizing the Microsoft Entra Connect Sync at *https://aka.ms/ SC900_EntraConnectCustomize*.

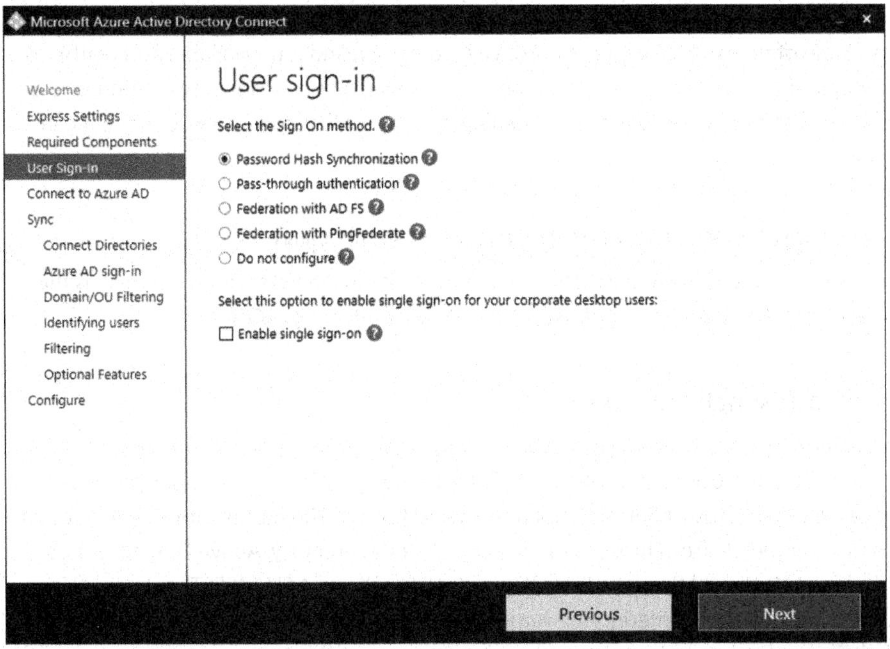

FIGURE 2-1 User sign-in options

Microsoft Entra cloud sync

Microsoft Entra Cloud sync is the latest tool used to create users, groups, and contacts in Microsoft Entra ID. It is similar to Microsoft Entra Connect. The primary difference is that a lightweight agent is used, as shown in Figure 2-2, and the cloud sync configuration is entirely managed in the cloud.

This sync agent setup works well for Active Directory multi-forest setups that are disconnected from each other. For example, during a merger and acquisition scenario, the on-prem Active Directory forests would typically not have any network connectivity to each other. Multiple Entra Cloud Sync agents can provide a high-availability sync and run side by side with Microsoft Entra Connect.

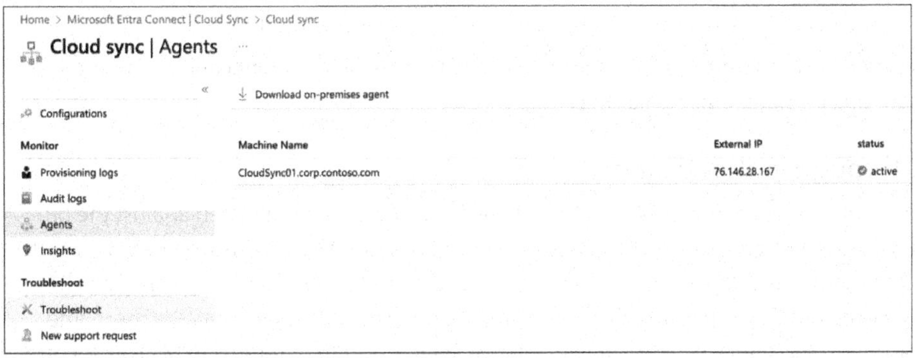

FIGURE 2-2 Cloud Sync agents

Not all functionality in Microsoft Entra Connect is available yet in Microsoft Entra Cloud sync. At the time of this writing, support for device object syncing is unavailable and neither is syncing groups with more than 250,000 members. However, new functionality continues to be added to Microsoft Entra Cloud Sync. If you can use this over Microsoft Entra Connect, it can simplify your hybrid setup.

> **MORE INFO MICROSOFT ENTRA CHOOSE THE RIGHT SYNC CLIENT**
>
> You can read more about the functionality supported in Microsoft Entra cloud sync versus the same in Microsoft Entra Connect at *https://aka.ms/SC900_ChooseSyncClient*.

Password hash synchronization

The current credentials in on-premises Active Directory are synced to Microsoft Entra ID through Microsoft Entra Connect or Microsoft Entra Cloud Sync. The on-premises password itself is never sent to Microsoft Entra ID, but a password hash is. The hashes stored in Microsoft Entra ID differ completely from those in on-premises Active Directory. Active Directory password hashes are MD4, and Microsoft Entra ID password hashes are SHA256. The user authenticates to Microsoft Entra ID, entering the same password they use on-premises. See the next More Info item for the detailed cryptographic specifics on how this process works.

> **MORE INFO MICROSOFT ENTRA CONNECT PASSWORD HASH SYNC DETAILS**
>
> You can read more about the Microsoft Entra Connect Sync Password Hash Sync at *http://aka.ms/SC900_HowPHSWorks*.

You can also select password hash sync as an optional feature in Microsoft Entra Connect if you use pass-through authentication (PTA) or federation as your primary authentication method, as shown in Figure 2-3. This gives you two benefits:

- Microsoft Entra can alert you when the username and password are discovered online. There will be a leaked credential alert for that user.
- If something catastrophic happens to the on-premises Active Directory, an admin can flip the authentication method to password hash sync. This would allow users to access cloud resources when the full disaster recovery plan is executed.

Password hash synchronization should be used as the default authentication choice unless there are specific requirements not to do so.

Pass-through authentication

Pass-through authentication (PTA) allows the user's password to be validated against the on-premises Active Directory using PTA agents. When a user goes to authentication to Microsoft Entra, the username and password are encrypted and put into a queue. The on-premises PTA agent reaches outbound to Microsoft Entra ID, picks up the request, decrypts the username and password, and then validates it against Active Directory. It then returns to Microsoft Entra ID if the authentication is successful. This allows for on-premises policies such as sign-in-hour restrictions to be evaluated during authentication to cloud services. The password hash doesn't need to be present in Microsoft Entra ID in any form for PTA authentication to work. However, PHS can be enabled as an optional feature.

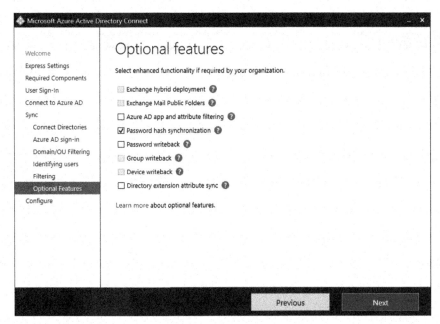

FIGURE 2-3 Password hash synchronization

The first PTA agent is usually installed on the Microsoft Entra Connect server. In a disconnected forest scenario, Microsoft Entra Cloud Sync does not support PTA authentication. It's recommended that you have a minimum of three PTA agents for redundancy. You can see the total number of PTA agents installed at the Microsoft Entra Connect page in the Microsoft Entra ID Portal, which is shown in Figure 2-4.

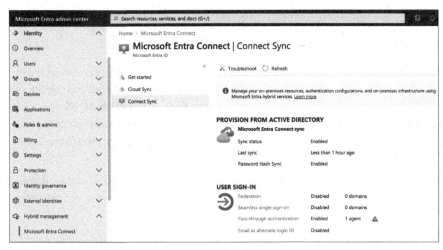

FIGURE 2-4 Pass-through authentication agent installed

To see the specific IPs of the PTA agents, click **Pass-Through Authentication**, as shown in Figure 2-5. The maximum number of PTA agents per tenant is 40. The servers running PTA agents should also be treated and protected the same as you would protect a domain controller.

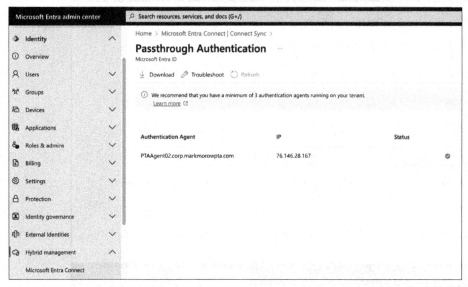

FIGURE 2-5 Pass-through authentication agent details

PTA should be used as an authentication choice if password hash sync cannot be used or if sign-in hour restrictions are required. Also, PTA is useful for a company trying to move away from federated authentication that doesn't want to move to password hash sync yet.

> **MORE INFO PASS-THROUGH AUTHENTICATION**
>
> You can learn more about the details of how PTA works at *https://aka.ms/SC900_PTADeepDive*.

Federation

This allows users to authenticate to Microsoft Entra ID resources using credentials provided by another identity provider (IdP). Active Directory Federation Services is installed and configured in the Microsoft Entra Connect setup when you choose the **Federation With AD FS** option. Also, a Web Application Proxy (WAP) server is installed to facilitate communication between the on-premises AD FS deployment and the Internet. The WAP should be located in the DMZ. The AD FS server should never be exposed to the Internet directly.

Federation is the most complicated identity authentication configuration. There are a few reasons why federated authentication to Microsoft Entra ID would be needed, and doing so should be the last choice when evaluating PHS, PTA, and federation.

Finally, AD FS servers should be protected and treated the same way as domain controllers. If an attacker could access the AD FS server, they could sign claims impersonating any user in the directory.

MORE INFO **CHOOSING THE RIGHT AUTHORIZATION METHOD FOR YOUR HYBRID IDENTITY**

If you are unsure which method is best for you, follow the decision tree located at *https://aka.ms/SC900_ChooseTheRightAuthN*.

EXAM TIP

Make sure to understand what a hybrid identity is and the associated components used in a hybrid identity configuration.

Describe Microsoft Entra identities (users, devices, groups, and workload identities)

Microsoft Entra identities comprise four main categories of identities: users, devices, groups, and workload identities, which can thought of as an application identity. All of these will be present in your Microsoft Entra tenant.

Users

User identities are typically connected to a person. You traditionally think of these identities when users authenticate to a resource. When someone starts working at a company, they are given a user identity to identify the user across various applications and services, such as O365 or external SaaS applications. User identities can be added to groups or distribution lists and hold administrative roles. Authorization decisions are made against user identities. User identities can be members of your organization or outside of your organization.

As covered in the "Describe what hybrid identity is" section, user identities are most typically synced from on-premises Active Directory via Microsoft Entra Cloud Sync or Microsoft Entra Connect. The user's attributes, such as name, department, and office phone, can all be synced in Microsoft Entra Cloud Sync or Microsoft Entra Connect.

User identities can also be created directly in Microsoft Entra ID. An on-premises Active Directory is not needed. The population of additional user data, such as department, is still needed. Another system usually provides this as part of user onboarding. Both user identity types are shown in Figure 2-6.

NOTE When the term *identity* is used, it most likely refers to a user identity.

FIGURE 2-6 All users in Microsft Entra, including synced and cloud-only users

Devices

Devices also have an identity in Microsoft Entra. There are three types of device identities in Microsoft Entra ID, but we also included a fourth identity type, an on-premises device identity, so you have a complete picture of all device states you will encounter.

- **Domain–joined computer**   First, we have a traditional domain-joined computer. This is usually a corporate-owned device joined to the on-premises Active Directory. The on-premises Active Directory account is used to sign-in. This is probably the device identity type you are the most familiar with because it has been used since Active Directory first arrived in Windows 2000.

- **Microsoft Entra Hybrid–joined device**   Next, there is the Microsoft Entra Hybrid–joined device, which is where the device is domain-joined to Active Directory but also has an identity in Microsoft Entra. Typically, this identity is created through the Microsoft Entra Connect sync process when syncing computer accounts to Microsoft Entra ID. The account used to log in to the device is still an on-premises Active Directory account. However, because this device has an identity in Microsoft Entra ID, this can be used as part of the conditional access controls. It also gives users a better user experience by reducing prompts for Microsoft Entra ID–backed applications.

- **Microsoft Entra–joined**   Microsoft Entra–joined devices are directly joined to Microsoft Entra ID. Instead of being domain-joined to on-premises Active Directory, it's joined directly to Microsoft Entra ID. Microsoft Intune applies policy and manages the Microsoft Entra–joined device. With a Microsoft Entra–joined device, the Microsoft Entra account is used to log in. A device cannot be domain joined to both Active Directory and Entra ID at the same time.

- **Microsoft Entra–registered**   Typically, this is a personal device, such as a mobile phone or a personally owned computer. This is mostly used for BYOD scenarios where some corporate resources are needed, but a device is not provided. Microsoft Intune is used to provide some light management capabilities. A local account, perhaps a

Microsoft account, is used to log in rather than a corporate Active Directory or Microsoft Entra account. Microsoft Entra–joined, Microsoft Entra hybrid–joined, and Microsoft Entra–registered can all be seen in the **Devices** section of the Microsoft Entra admin center, as shown in Figure 2-7.

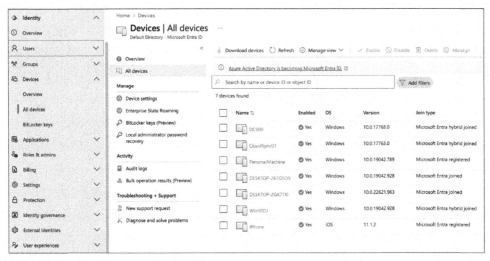

FIGURE 2-7 All devices in Microsoft Entra ID

Groups

Groups are a collection of users or devices. They are used to specify an action or apply a policy on many of these objects at once instead of doing it individually. For example, if we want to grant everyone in the sales department access to a sales application, we can assign the sales group instead of assigning each member individually. We can also apply licenses to the group; all members will receive the license assignment. This allows the admin to take actions at a greater scale.

There are several types of groups that you can use in Azure AD:

- You can sync your on-premises groups from Active Directory for use as a security group.

- You can also create a Microsoft Entra security group where the membership is assigned directly to the group.

- The group can also be made to be of a dynamic membership. This means membership will be automatically populated based on the user's attributes or the device you want in the group.

The different group types and membership types are shown in Figure 2-8.

Using the previous sales team example, a dynamic group could be made where when the department equals Sales, which means they are automatically in the group (see Figure 2-9). These dynamic groups are constantly reevaluating and adding and removing members. The automation that can be built around dynamic groups is tremendous.

FIGURE 2-8 New Group creation

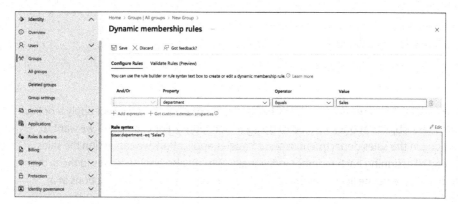

FIGURE 2-9 Dynamic Membership Rules

Microsoft 365 groups—sometimes called unified groups—are newer group types representing the future direction for resource permissions in Microsoft 365, such as Teams, SharePoint, and Exchange Online. One group can be used to ensure consistent access with minor administrative effort across the Microsoft 365 suite of applications.

Workload identities

Nobody logs into anything for the fun of it. Users log in to do something important to them, such as send an email, check their paystub, or access a line-of-business application. Applications are the day-to-day drivers for users, and many applications exist in Microsoft Entra ID. These will sometimes be referred to as a *workload identity*. There is no industry standard for this term; depending on the context, they can discuss a few different things. This can refer to an application, a service principal, a specific instance of an application, or a managed identity, a special type of service principal. All three of these will be covered in this section.

As described earlier, Microsoft Entra ID supports open standards such as SAML, OAuth, and OpenID Connect. Any applications that support these protocols can be integrated into Microsoft Entra ID. Microsoft Entra ID also has an Application Gallery where Microsoft has worked with these different application providers to make the setup as easy as possible. The Application Gallery can be seen in Figure 2-10. Microsoft Entra ID can also work with your on-premises web applications using Microsoft Entra Application Proxy, as described in the "Describe what Microsoft Entra ID is" section later in this chapter.

> **MORE INFO   MODERN AUTHENTICATION**
>
> To learn more about modern authentication, watch the Bailey, Bercik, and Mark Morowczynski session at Defcon Blue Team Village Modern Authorization for the Security Admin at *https://aka.ms/SC900_ModernAuthBTV*.

Line-of-business applications can also be updated to use Microsoft Entra authentication. Because Microsoft Entra ID supports open standards, any language that has a library for SAML, OAuth, or OpenID Connect can integrate with Microsoft Entra ID. Microsoft also has the MSAL library to simplify authentication for many common languages, such as .NET, ASP.NET, Node.js, Java, Python, iOS, macOS, Android, and Xamarin.

> **MORE INFO   MSAL LIBRARIES**
>
> To learn more about the MSAL libraries available, see *https://aka.ms/SC900_MSAL*.

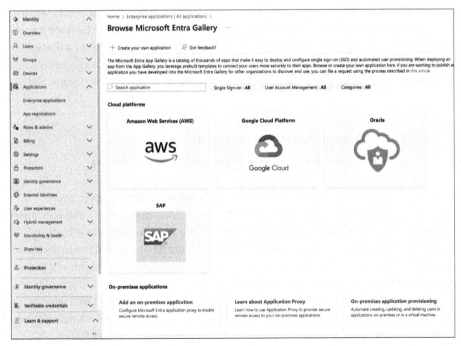

FIGURE 2-10 Microsoft Entra application gallery

Application identities can be seen in the Enterprise Apps section of the Microsoft Entra admin center, as shown in Figure 2-11. These are called *service principals*. These define the access policy and permissions for the application insofar as what it can do in the tenant. There is a lot of developer detail beyond the scope of this exam, but here is a real-world example: When applying a conditional access policy, such as requiring users to complete MFA before accessing an application, you apply a conditional access policy to a service principal. These are automatically added to the tenant when you integrate an application from the Application Gallery, consent to an application, or add an app proxy application.

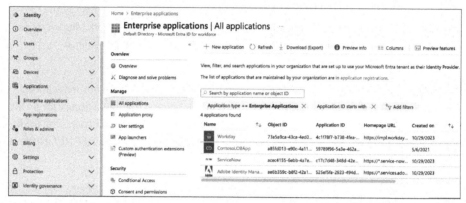

FIGURE 2-11 Microsoft Entra Enterprise Applications

A second type of service principal is called a *managed identity*. This is typically for developers, but it can really be used by anyone managing Azure resources that access Microsoft Entra authentication. The idea is that no credential management needs to be done for the application. Without managed identities, a developer would need to rotate either a shared secret (a password for an application) or a certificate at regular intervals. These credentials need to be protected as well. With a managed identity, the service handles the storage and rotation.

> **MORE INFO   MICROSOFT ENTRA MANAGED IDENTITIES**
>
> To learn more about Managed Identities, see *https://aka.ms/ManagedIdentities*.

The final type of application identity is the application object created by application registration. This configures the application to use Microsoft Entra identities for authentication (in your tenant or by other people's Microsoft Entra tenants if you choose to allow that) and results in an application object being created in Microsoft Entra ID. Things like the application uniform resource identifier (URI) and application permissions are defined in this object. Every application object (created through the Azure portal or by using the Microsoft Graph APIs or the Azure AD PS Module) also creates a corresponding service principal object that inherits certain properties from that application object. This is located in a tenant, but it would not be in your tenant unless it were an application your company was developing (see Figure 2-12).

FIGURE 2-12 Microsoft Entra Application Registration

Putting it all together with a few examples should clarify what administrators see in the portal. Contoso is using Office 365. There will be a service principal for Office 365 Exchange online, Office 365 SharePoint online, and so on in their Enterprise Apps. No application registration for those applications occurs. The application registration will happen in the Microsoft tenant, not the Contoso tenant. The only thing Contoso would see is the service principal in Enterprise Applications. This applies to any application added from the gallery or that is manually added. Contoso is moving its line-of-business application to leverage Microsoft Entra authentication. In this scenario, there would be an object for this line-of-business application in the Application Registrations section and a service principal object in the Enterprise Applications section.

> **MORE INFO** **MICROSOFT ENTRA APPLICATIONS AND SERVICE PRINCIPALS**
>
> To learn more about Microsoft Entra applications and service principals, see
> *https://aka.ms/SC900_ME-IDAppObjects*

Skill 2.2: Describe the authentication capabilities of Microsoft Entra ID

This objective deals with the authentication capabilities of Microsoft Entra ID. You will learn how you can prevent users from using weak passwords in your Microsoft Entra ID and Active Directory. Then, we'll focus on multifactor authentication—what it means, and what methods are available for users. Finally, we'll discuss passwordless and phishing-resistant authentication methods such as Hello for Business, certificate-based authentication, FIDO2, and the authenticator app, which significantly increase both security and the user experience.

> **This skill covers:**
> - Authentication methods, including passwords MFA
> - Learn about password protection and management
> - Multifactor authentication methods
> - Learn about passwordless credentials, which provide the best balance between user experience and security

Describe the different authentication methods

Microsoft Entra ID provides multiple authentication methods for users. The most common one is passwords. While many people are familiar with this method, we saw in the identity principles and concepts section that many of the most common attacks involve using passwords. Passwords must be strengthened where possible and paired with stronger factors until they can be removed entirely.

Later in this section, we'll go into more detail about MFA methods, but multifactor authentication is some combination of something you know, something you have, or something you are. The following factors satisfy the something you have requirement: a phone call, a text message, a hardware token, a software token with a one-time passcode (OTP), or a Microsoft Authenticator or Microsoft Authenticator Lite app push notification. Combining a password with one of these methods will greatly increase your security posture and is really the minimum-security bar organizations should reach in a modern environment.

The latest and strongest authentication methods are passwordless (a form of multifactor authentication that no longer requires a password); some are phishing-resistant. These include Windows Hello for Business, FIDO2, Certificate-based authentication, and the Microsoft Authenticator app. To register for a passwordless authentication, these credentials must be bootstrapped by leveraging MFA or a Temporary Access Pass (TAP). A TAP is a time-limited passcode issued by an admin and satisfies strong authentication requirements. A TAP can be used to register passwordless credentials.

In this section, we'll go into more detail about how we can strengthen passwords and MFA and even move to stronger authentication, such as passwordless credentials like Hello for Business.

Describe password protection and management capabilities

At this point, it should be obvious that passwords are one of the weakest security links we have in our organizations. As much as we'd like to remove passwords altogether, that isn't practical for most environments. However, there are several things we can do today to strengthen the passwords we use. First, the password policies set by organizations put people into predictable patterns for password use. As we saw with the password spray attack, having users change their passwords every 30 days can lead to users setting their password to the `MonthYearSpecialCharacter` (for example, `December2023!`) pattern. Often, quarterly password changes result in users creating passwords that match the seasons. This should be changed from a policy perspective to require stronger passwords that are changed less frequently.

Another way to stop these easily guessable passwords is to leverage Microsoft Entra Password Protection, which detects and prevents easily known passwords from being used through a global banned list, which is a custom list that an organization controls and uses a scoring-based system. Microsoft Entra Password Protection can be set in Audit or Enforced mode, which allows you to see how many passwords would have been blocked. This is a great way to show the need for enabling features with management. It works natively for cloud-based accounts and can be extended to on-premises accounts in Active Directory!

MORE INFO **ORGANIZATIONAL PASSWORD POLICIES**

For recommendations on password management, see *https://aka.ms/SC900_PasswordGuidance.*

Microsoft Entra Password Protection Global Banned List

The global banned list is updated and maintained by the Microsoft Entra team and is based on commonly used weak or compromised passwords. There is nothing to configure, update, or maintain from an organizational perspective. This list cannot be disabled either. This list is automatically applied during a password change or reset through Microsoft Entra ID. When passwords are evaluated, this list will automatically be combined with the custom banned list.

Microsoft Entra Password Protection Custom Banned List

The custom banned list enables organizations to add "banned" passwords specific to their organization. This should include things like product and brand names, company locations, and company-specific internal terms or abbreviations. It's also good to add passwords that have local significance, such as local sports teams (see Figure 2-13). This list can hold a maximum number of 1,000 terms. The custom list is not meant to hold a large common password list like the i rockyou list. Remember, the passwords must pass a scoring threshold. They are not banned outright just because they appear on the list.

NOTE **IROCKYOU LIST**

The i rockyou list is a large list of commonly used passwords. Attackers use this list when attempting to guess a password.

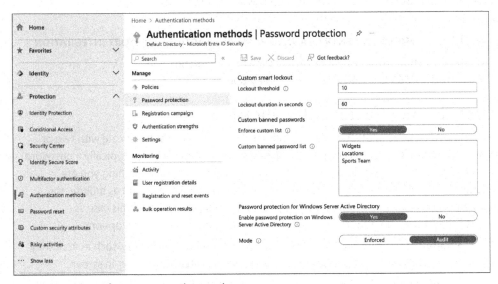

FIGURE 2-13 Microsoft Entra Password protection

How passwords are scored

Passwords go through several steps during the scoring process. First, they go through a normalization process. All uppercase characters are changed to lowercase, and all common character substitutions are performed (for example, in p@ssw0rd, the @ is changed to the letter a, and 0 (zero) is changed to a letter o). Then, the score for the password is calculated. First, fuzzy matching and substring matching are performed to see if the normalized password appears on the global or custom banned password list. For each banned password in the global or custom list found to be part of the user's password, one point is given. Then, one point is given for each remaining character not part of the banned password. A password must get a score of 5 or above to be accepted.

> **MORE INFO   PASSWORD SCORING EXAMPLES**
>
> For more examples of the scoring process, see *https://aka.ms/SC900_PasswordScoring*.

Microsoft Entra Password Protection with Active Directory

Microsoft Entra Password Protection can also be used with on-premises Active Directory. The same global and custom list can be used for password resets or changes in Active Directory. At a high level, a password protection agent that includes a password filter .dll is installed on each domain controller. This will also work with any existing password filters on the domain controller. This agent contacts the Microsoft Entra Password Protection Proxy service running on a domain member server. This protection proxy member server contacts Microsoft Entra ID to get the global and custom lists. You can now apply the same global and custom list to password changes or resets in Microsoft Entra ID or Active Directory. This is a great way to increase your password strength across both on-premises and in the cloud.

> **MORE INFO   MICROSOFT ENTRA BANNED PASSWORD ACTIVE DIRECTORY INTEGRATION**
>
> For details on how to implement the Active Directory integration, see *https://aka.ms/SC900_BannedPasswordADIntegration*.

Describe multifactor authentication

As described earlier, multifactor authentication requires a user to authenticate with two or more different factor types. These factor types are something you know (typically a password), something you have (typically a phone or other physical device), or something you are (biometrics). Having a user enter two different passwords would not count as multifactor authentication because passwords use the same type of factor, which, in this case, is knowledge. Microsoft Entra MFA includes several different authentication options.

- **Phone**   The user will get a phone call and must press a specific key, such as #, or they will get an SMS text message containing a code to enter into the log-in screen.
- **Mobile app notification**   The Microsoft Authenticator application receives a push notification from Microsoft Entra MFA. The user sees the notification in which they must

verify their authentication. The user approves it if the user performed the authentication or denies it otherwise. Users who do not have the Microsoft Authenticator app but have Microsoft Outlook Mobile will be able to use the Authenticator Lite. MFA push notifications are sent to Outlook.

- **Mobile app code/Software Tokens** The Microsoft Authenticator app supports the Open Authentication (OATH) time-based, one-time password (TOTP) standard. The code rotates every 30 or 60 seconds. Other software tokens that support OATH-TOTP can also be used, as well as any other software authenticator apps that support OATH-TOTP.

- **Hardware Tokens** OATH-TOTP SHA-1 tokens that refresh every 30 or 60 seconds can also be used.

- **Certificate-based authentication** For those with existing PKI infrastructure, a certificate or a smart card can be used.

These multifactor authentication methods and the passwordless methods covered in the next section are completely configurable when it comes to who is allowed to register and the method they may use (see Figure 2-14). For example, perhaps you want your administrators and users with access to sensitive information to use only phishing-resistant methods. You can scope them so they can only use those, but everyone else can continue using Hardware OATH tokens.

FIGURE 2-14 Microsoft Entra Authentication method policies

To require users to perform Microsoft Entra MFA when accessing a resource, make sure to configure the option in conditional access. (This will be covered in Skill 2.3.) Applications that leverage modern protocols such as WS-Fed, SAML, OAuth, and OpenID Connect and are integrated with Microsoft Entra ID can require MFA before access. Also, applications connected to Microsoft Entra ID through Microsoft Entra Application Proxy can leverage Microsoft Entra MFA because the user performs MFA against Microsoft Entra ID before accessing the application. This means the application doesn't need to make any changes to take advantage of Microsoft Entra MFA or any other conditional access controls.

Finally, be mindful of over-prompting users. This can lead to MFA fatigue, where they mistakenly accept an MFA prompt generated by an attacker, which defeats the purpose of MFA altogether. Another method is to leverage a passwordless technology like Windows Hello For business or FIDO2 at sign-in to the workstation. Doing so would satisfy any future MFA prompts because strong authentication is performed at sign-in. MFA is the bare minimum that can be done today, but the direction you should be moving toward is passwordless authentication. It's the strongest form of authentication and provides the best user experience. It's truly a win-win.

EXAM TIP

Make sure you understand what makes up MFA and the methods that can be used for MFA authentication (phone, text, Authenticator app, Authenticator Lite, and a hardware token).

Describe Windows Hello for Business and passwordless credentials

Passwordless credentials are the latest form of strong authentication, providing the best balance between user experience and security. They authenticate the user by combining MFA methods—something you have (the device), something you know (in this case, a PIN tied to the physical device), or something you are (biometrics). Biometrics include fingerprint or facial recognition.

NOTE PIN VERSUS PASSWORD

The important thing to understand that separates a PIN from a password is that a PIN can only be used on the device where it's registered. A password could be used anywhere. This is a huge security improvement because knowing the PIN is only valuable to the attacker if they have that specific device.

Also, because the user is performing MFA on sign-in to the device, their authentication token will reflect that they've already completed MFA. That means future MFA challenges are automatically satisfied when this token is used, drastically reducing the MFA prompts the user would normally see without compromising the security. This makes for a great user experience and prevents over-prompting for MFA. Microsoft Entra ID has four types of passwordless credentials: Windows Hello for Business, Microsoft Authenticator app, FIDO2, and certificates.

Windows Hello for Business is a great passwordless solution for a user using the same device daily. Think of your traditional information worker assigned a workstation only they use. To use Windows Hello for Business, a user must complete Windows Hello for Business registration, as shown in Figure 2-15, by performing strong authentication. During this registration process, the user would create their PIN and optionally enroll in biometrics, such as fingerprint or facial recognition, if the device hardware supports it and is configured to do so by the administrator. A public/private key is also generated, with the private key being stored in the Trust Platform Module (TPM) chip. The user logs in by either entering their PIN or using a biometric method.

This act unlocks the TPM chip to access the private key. Windows then uses the private key to authenticate the user with Microsoft Entra ID.

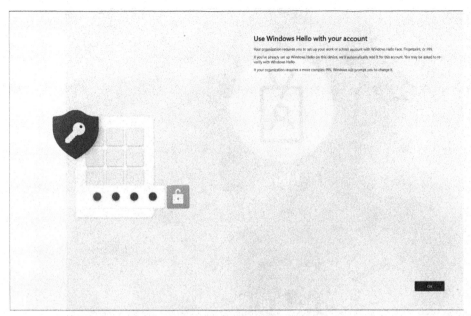

FIGURE 2-15 Windows Hello for Business registration screen

There are two important things to understand about this process:

- **The PIN and biometrics (if used) never leave the device.**   They aren't stored in Microsoft Entra ID and do not roam to any other devices. They are completely local to the device where registration took place.

- **The PIN and biometrics are not used to authenticate the user to Microsoft Entra ID.**   This is a common misconception. The private key is used to do the authentication. The PIN and biometrics unlock the TPM to access the private key. The private key (protected by the TPM) authenticates the user to Microsoft Entra ID, NOT the PIN or biometric.

The user sign-in experience is shown in Figure 2-16.

MORE INFO **WINDOWS HELLO FOR BUSINESS**

To understand the finer details of the Windows Hello for Business registration and authentication process, see *https://aka.ms/SC900_H4BDeepDive*.

The second passwordless factor is the Microsoft Authenticator app, which works well when the user is using a noncorporate device, such as a personal/home machine, mobile phone, or a non-Windows device (Mac or Linux workstation). The user must have the Microsoft Authenticator installed on their mobile device. They then complete the enable phone sign-in process in the Authenticator app. The phone sign-in process requires a user to match the number on the screen at sign-in, as shown in Figure 2-17, by typing the number on the device, as shown in Figure 2-18.

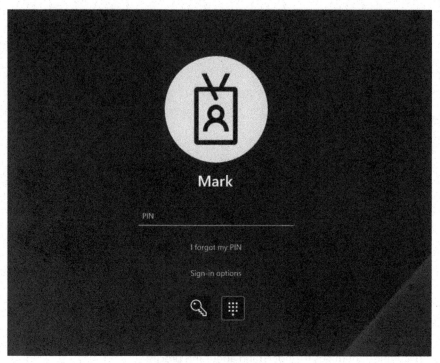

FIGURE 2-16 Windows log-in screen with the Windows Hello for Business PIN

FIGURE 2-17 Passwordless number match sign-in seen by the user.

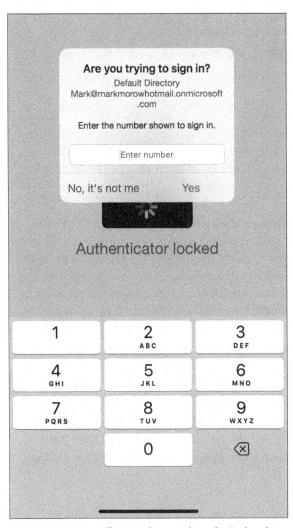

FIGURE 2-18 Passwordless number match on the Authenticator app

Next, we have the FIDO2 credentials, an open standard supported by the FIDO alliance. FIDO2 authentication works best in a one-to-many machine scenario or where mobile phones are not allowed for safety or security reasons. For example, a manufacturing floor might have a handful of machines for workers to log hours, check benefits, or check email. They might use a different machine each time. They also may not be allowed to bring in a mobile phone. FIDO2 has many different form factors of devices besides the traditional USB key, such as RFID badges. FIDO2 registration and authentication work very similarly to Windows Hello for Business, except the private key is stored on the FIDO2 device itself (rather than on the TPM of the computer). As with the TPM, this private key is designed never to be exported from that FIDO2 device.

MORE INFO FIDO ALLIANCE AND FIDO2 SPECIFICATIONS

To learn more about the FIDO Alliance members and the protocol details of FIDO2, see *https://aka.ms/SC900_FIDO2*.

EXAM TIP

The Hello for Business biometrics and PIN never leave the device. They are not stored in Microsoft Entra ID or any other device. They are only stored on the device on which Hello for Business registration was completed.

Finally, we have the certificate-based authentication as a passwordless method, which is useful if an organization already has a PKI setup where users use smart cards to authenticate. The details of how this works are outside the scope of this book, but fundamentally, there is a private-public key relationship where the private key is stored securely on a physical device, and certificates are issued from a certificate authority. There is a registration process to get these certificates, which may happen automatically or require some in-person offline activity or proofing to occur.

Certificate authentication can be configured to be a first factor and then combined with the authenticator app or a FIDO2 security key to achieve a login without using passwords and still meeting multifactor requirements.

Certificate-based authentication can also be configured as multifactor authentication by mapping to the issuer subject or policy OID files in the certificate. This is set up by an administrator and typically aligned with how the certificate was issued following NIST 800-64B. However, administrators should ensure the certificates are protected with a PIN or a hardware module.

MORE INFO NIST AUTHENTICATION ASSURANCE LEVELS AND MICROSOFT ENTRA ID

To learn more about which authentication methods meet NIST AAL levels, see *https://aka.ms/SC900_NISTAAL*.

Throughout this section, we've used the term *phishing-resistant authentication method*. At the time of this writing, all phishing-resistant methods are passwordless, but not all passwordless methods are phishing-resistant. A common phishing attack to capture credentials is getting a user to go visit a page that the adversary controls and can be in between the communication between the end user and the service. This is known as an adversary in the middle. They intercept the traffic in both directions and essentially authenticate as that user to the service.

What makes an authentication method resistant to phishing is that in the authentication flow, Microsoft Entra ID will use a cryptographic nonce that is encrypted with the end user's public key that no one can decrypt but the user with that private key. Continue to check the public documentation on phishing-resistant methods for the latest and continue to move your organization to use the strongest possible credentials whenever possible.

The following passwordless credentials meet this criteria at the time of this writing:

- Windows Hello For Business
- FIDO2 Security keys
- Certificate-based authorization

> **MORE INFO** **TO LEARN MORE ABOUT HOW PHISHING-RESISTANT**
>
> To learn more about how phishing-resistant methods work under the covers, watch this excellent session by Inbar Cizer Kobrinsky and Tarek Dawoud at *https://aka.ms/ SC900_PhishingResistantDeepDive.*

Skill 2.3: Describe the access management capabilities of Microsoft Entra ID

This objective deals with the access management capabilities of Microsoft Entra ID. Conditional access is the main driver of access in Microsoft Entra ID. You'll learn the different configuration options available in conditional access and common conditional access policies. You'll also learn about the built-in Microsoft Entra ID roles and following the least-privilege model.

> **This skill covers:**
> - Understand conditional access
> - Uses and benefits of conditional access
> - Microsoft Entra roles and role-based access

Describe what conditional access is

Conditional access is the main decision engine, enforcement point, and the ultimate driver of identity as the primary security perimeter, as discussed in the "Identity principles and concepts" section. As an administrator, you can combine different requirements, such as who the user is, groups or roles they belong to, what type of device they are coming from, which application they are using, what the user risk level is, and where they are coming from to determine if they are allowed access, denied access, or must perform additional authentication like multifactor authentication or must use a specific type of multifactor strength before they can access the resource.

These checks are performed each time a new authentication is performed against Microsoft Entra ID. A denied message is shown in Figure 2-19, which will be displayed if the authentication attempt does not meet the requirements of the conditional access policy.

Conditional access also works with other Microsoft 365 features, such as Microsoft Cloud Application Security (MCAS) for additional security to monitor sessions and activities performed within that session after authentication. Conditional access gives administrators great flexibility to ensure that the organization's assets and resources are protected at the security levels desired. Conditional access also ensures that the workforce can still work at any time and wherever they are.

FIGURE 2-19 Conditional access policy message when the policy requirements are not met

Describe uses and benefits of conditional access

Conditional access gives the administrator very granular control to ensure users meet the organization's security requirements to access Microsoft Entra ID –protected resources. There are many different configuration choices to meet various scenarios (see Figure 2-20).

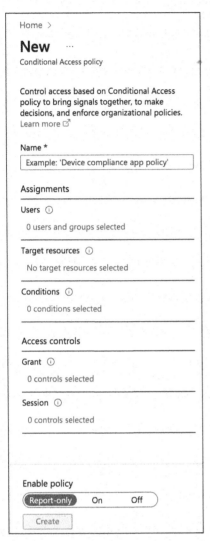

FIGURE 2-20 Conditional Access Policy options

The configuration options shown in Figure 2-20 are as shown here:

- **Name** A name for the conditional access policy
- **Users** Users, groups, or roles the policy applies to. This includes guests or external users and the ability to exclude users, groups, or roles from the policy.
- **Target resources** The cloud apps or user actions the policy applies to. Policies can apply to some or all applications. This includes applications you have tagged with custom security attributes or have an authentication context set. For example, there might be a resource with sensitive data to which you want to apply stricter security controls. You can also specify specific user actions that trigger the conditional access policy, such as registering for multifactor authentication or joining a device to Microsoft Entra ID.

- **Conditions** The conditions in which the associated policy will apply. These include user and sign-in risk, which we will cover more specifically in Skill 2.4, "Describe the identity protection and governance capabilities of Microsoft Entra."

    - You can determine the device platforms the policy will apply to, such as Windows, Android, iOS, macOS, or Linux.

    - You can determine which location the policy should apply to if you are coming from off the corporate network or a specific geographic location configured in your **Named Networks** settings.

    - You can determine which client apps this policy will apply to. Does it apply to modern authentication clients like browsers, mobile apps, and desktop clients? Or does this policy apply to legacy authentication clients like ActiveSync?

    - You can determine the device state to which this policy applies, such as whether the device is Microsoft Entra hybrid AD–joined or marked as compliant.

    - You can also target or exclude specific devices in the environment using filters for devices.

- **Access Controls** This can be a block control that would prevent access if the policy were applied, or it can be a grant control if the user passes the controls specified. These grant controls include

    - Requiring the user to satisfy MFA.

    - Requiring a specific authentication strength such as passwordless credentials or a phishing resistant factor such as Windows Hello For Business, FIDO2, or certificate-based authentication.

    - Access from a Microsoft Intune–compliant device.

    - Access from a Microsoft Entra Hybrid–joined device.

    - For mobile use, an approved client app that does modern authentication, such as Outlook Mobile.

    - For mobile use, an app protection policy means the application is mobile application managed (MAM) in Microsoft Intune, preventing corporate data from being moved to noncorporate resources. For example, you cannot save an attached Word document from your corporate email to a personal OneDrive account; it can only be saved to a corporate OneDrive account.

    - Force the user to perform a password change. This is used with the user risk score.

- Session controls that can enable limited user experience with specific cloud applications, such as

    - App-enforced restrictions that limit what can be done in Exchange Online and Share-Point Online. For example, if you are coming from a noncorporate device, you can only read items on SharePoint Online but cannot download them.

    - Conditional access app control, which works with MCAS to monitor the session to prevent data exfiltration, protect sensitive data on download with Azure Information Protection, monitor for compliance, and block access altogether.

- Sign-in frequency defines the amount of time before a user is asked to sign in again when attempting to access a resource.

- A persistent browser session enables a user to remain signed in after closing and reopening their browser window.

- Customized continuous access evaluation can be used to disable this default functionality of longer-lived tokens that can be revoked nearly instantly for apps such as Exchange Online and SharePoint Online for all users, specific users, or groups. This also allows an administrator to strictly enforce policy locations, such as saying you can only access if you are coming from the corporate network space you've defined in **Named Locations**.

- Disabling resilience defaults allows an administrator to choose not to extend existing sessions while enforcing conditional access during a Microsoft Entra ID outage. At the end of the session, access will be denied.

- Require token protection for sign-in sessions, often referred to as *token binding*, attempts to reduce token theft by ensuring a token is usable from the intended device. This is an emerging area, so read the documentation to understand what specific platforms and applications this setting supports.

- **Enable Policy**   Can be set to **Report Only**, which you should use to determine how the policy will function before enforcing it (enabling or disabling the policy).

EXAM TIP

Make sure you understand the different configuration options when configuring a conditional access policy and what controls can be enforced on access.

Multiple policies can be created. When a user signs in, all policies are applied. There is no preference order when it comes to conditional access policies. Planning and forethought should be used to strike the correct balance of securing the resources, enabling users to access resources, and not having so many policies that management becomes unwieldy and confusing.

MORE INFO   **CONDITIONAL ACCESS POLICY PLANNING**

To learn more about planning your conditional access deployment and best practices, see *https://aka.ms/SC900_CAPlanning*.

Following are some common policies that many organizations tend to configure. There are 16 Conditional Access templates precreated for you in the following categories:

- **Secure foundations**
  - Require MFA for Administrators
  - Securing security info registration
  - Block legacy authentication

- Require MFA for all users
- Require MFA for admins accessing Microsoft admin portals
- Require MFA for Azure management
- Require compliant or Microsoft Entra Hybrid–joined device or MFA for all users

- **Zero Trust**
  - Require MFA for Administrators
  - Securing security info registration
  - Block legacy authentication
  - Require MFA for all users
  - Require MFA for guest access
  - Require MFA for Azure management
  - Require MFA for risky sign-ins
  - Require password change for high-risk users
  - Block access for unknown or unsupported device platform
  - No persistent browser session
  - Require approved client apps or app protection policies
  - Require a compliant or Microsoft Entra Hybrid–joined device or MFA for all users
  - Require MFA for admins accessing Microsoft admin portals

- **Remote Work**
  - Securing security info registration
  - Block legacy authentication
  - Require MFA for all users
  - Require MFA for guest access
  - Require MFA for risky sign-ins
  - Require password change for high-risk users
  - Require compliant or Microsoft Entra Hybrid–joined device or MFA for administrators
  - Block access for unknown or unsupported device platform
  - No persistent browser session
  - Require approved client apps or app protection policies
  - Use application-enforced restrictions for unmanaged devices

- **Protect administrator**
  - Require MFA for admins
  - Block legacy authentication
  - Require MFA for Azure management

- Require a compliant or Microsoft Entra Hybrid–joined device or MFA for administrators
- Require phishing-resistant MFA for administrators
- **Emerging threats**
  - Require phishing-resistant MFA for administrators

> ***MORE INFO*** **CONDITIONAL ACCESS RECOMMENDED POLICIES**
>
> For recommended conditional access policies across Microsoft 365, see *https://aka.ms/* Microsoft 365*goldenconfig*.

Describe Microsoft Entra roles and role-based access control (RBAC)

Microsoft Entra ID has many built-in roles that allow the holder of that role to perform Microsoft Entra ID management tasks that a regular user cannot perform (see Figure 2-21). The concept of assigning permissions based on an individual's role is known as role-based access control (RBAC). This is less error-prone than assigning permissions to a user individually. This also makes it easy when a user changes jobs; they can be removed from that role, and those permissions would no longer be available to them. People should be assigned roles that satisfy the least-privilege they need to complete the task. Following the least-privilege model is one of three Zero Trust principles.

For example, if someone needs to administer the devices in Microsoft Entra ID for the organization, they should use the **Cloud Device Administrator** role, not the **Global Administrator** role. Though the **Global Administrator** role has the permissions needed to manage devices, it has far more privileges than necessary to manage devices. This additional (unneeded) privilege could increase the damage of an inadvertent mistake by the admin or the damage of a compromised account by an attacker.

A good analogy is to think about the way a submarine is designed. A leak in one area of the hull is contained to that area and doesn't sink the entire ship. Roles following the principle of least-privilege work in a similar matter. The **Cloud Device Administrator** role cannot delete the directory like a **Global Administrator** can. Always follow the principle of least-privilege. The following built-in roles exist in Microsoft Entra ID:

- **Application Administrator**   Can create and manage all aspects of app registration and enterprise apps
- **Application Developer**   Can create application registrations independent of the **Users Can Register Applications** setting
- **Attack Payload Author**   Can create attack payloads that an administrator can initiate later
- **Attack Simulation Administrator**   Can create and manage all aspects of attack simulation campaigns

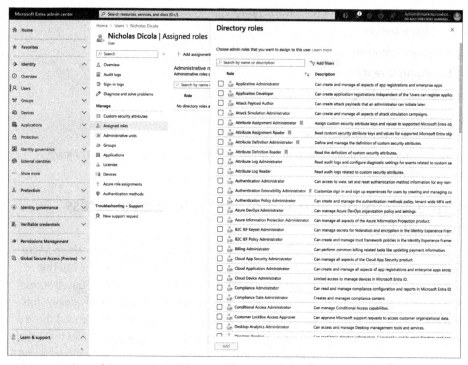

FIGURE 2-21 Microsoft Entra Roles available to assign to the user

- **Attribute Assignment Administrator**   Assign customer security attribute keys and values to supported Microsoft Entra objects

- **Attribute Assignment Reader**   Read custom security attribute keys and values for supported Microsoft Entra Objects

- **Attribute Definition Administrator**   Define and manage the definition of custom security attributes

- **Attribute Definition Reader**   Read the definition of a custom security attributes

- **Authentication Administrator**   Can access the view, set, and reset authentication method information for any nonadmin user

- **Authentication Policy Administrator**   Can create and manage all aspects of authentication methods and password protection policies

- **Azure AD Joined Device Local Administrator**   Users assigned to this role are added to the local administrators' group on Microsoft Entra–joined devices.

- **Azure DevOps Administrator**   Can manage Azure DevOps organization policy and settings

- **Azure Information Protection Administrator**   Can manage all aspects of the Azure Information Protection product

- **B2C IEF Keyset Administrator**   Can manage secrets for federation and encryption in the Identity Experience Framework (IEF)

- **B2C IEF Policy Administrator** Can create and manage trust framework policies in the Identity Experience Framework (IEF)
- **Billing Administrator** Can perform common billing-related tasks like updating payment information
- **Cloud App Security Administrator** Can manage all aspects of the Defender for Cloud Apps product
- **Cloud Application Administrator** Can create and manage all aspects of app registrations and enterprise apps except App Proxy
- **Cloud Device Administrator** Limited access to manage devices in Azure AD
- **Compliance Administrator** Can read and manage compliance configuration and reports in Azure AD and Microsoft 365
- **Compliance Data Administrator** Creates and manages compliance content
- **Conditional Access Administrator** Can manage conditional access capabilities
- **Customer LockBox Access Approver** Can approve Microsoft support requests to access customer organizational data
- **Desktop Analytics Administrator** Can access and manage desktop management tools and services
- **Directory Readers** Can read basic directory information. Commonly used to grant directory read access to applications and guests
- **Directory Synchronization Accounts** Only used by the Azure AD Connect service
- **Directory Writers** Can read and write basic directory information and are used for granting access to applications (not intended for users)
- **Domain Name Administrator** Can manage domain names in the cloud and on-premises
- **Dynamics 365 Administrator** Can manage all aspects of the Dynamics 365 product
- **Edge Administrator** Can manage all aspects of Microsoft Edge
- **Exchange Administrator** Can manage all aspects of the Exchange product
- **Exchange Recipient Administrator** Can create or update Exchange Online recipients within the Exchange Online organization
- **External ID User Flow Administrator** Can create and manage all aspects of user flows
- **External ID User Flow Attribute Administrator** Can create and manage the attribute schema available to all user flows
- **External Identity Provider Administrator** Can configure identity providers for the user in a direct federation
- **Fabric Administrator** Can manage all aspects of the Fabric and Power BI products
- **Global Administrator** Can manage all aspects of Azure AD and Microsoft services that use Azure AD identities

- **Global Reader**   Can read everything that a Global Administrator can but cannot update anything
- **Global Secure Access Administrator**   Can create and manage all aspects of Microsoft Entra Internet Access and Microsoft Entra Private Access, including managing access to public and private endpoints
- **Groups Administrator**   Members of this role can create/manage groups, create/manage group settings like naming and expiration policies, and view groups' activity and audit reports
- **Guest Inviter**   Can invite guest users independent of the **Members Can Invite Guests** setting
- **Helpdesk Administrator**   Can reset passwords for nonadministrators and Helpdesk Administrators
- **Hybrid Identity Administrator**   Can manage AD to Azure AD cloud provisioning, Azure AD Connect, and federation settings
- **Identity Governance Administrator**   Can manage access using Microsoft Entra ID for identity governance scenarios
- **Insights Administrator**   Has administrative access to the Microsoft 365 Insights app
- **Insights Analyst**   Access the analytical capabilities in Microsoft Viva Insights and run custom queries.
- **Insights Business Leader**   Can view and share dashboards and insights via the Microsoft 365 insights app
- **Microsoft Intune Administrator**   Can manage all aspects of the Microsoft Intune product
- **Kaizala Administrator**   Can manage settings for Microsoft Kaizala
- **Knowledge Administrator**   Can configure knowledge, learning, and other intelligent features
- **Knowledge Manager**   Can organize, create, manage, and promote topics and knowledge
- **License Administrator**   Can manage product licenses on users and groups
- **Lifecycle Workflow Aministrator**   Can create and manage all aspects of workflows and tasks associated with Lifecycle Workflows in Microsoft Entra ID
- **Message Center Privacy Reader**   Can read security messages and updates in the Office 365 Message Center only
- **Message Center Reader**   Can read messages and updates for their organization in Office 365 Message Center only
- **Modern Commerce User**   Can manage commercial purchases for a company, department, or team

- **Microsoft Hardware Warranty Administrator** Can create and manage all aspects of warranty claims and entitlements for Microsoft-manufactured hardware, like Surface and HoloLens

- **Microsoft Hardware Warranty Specialist** Can create and read warranty claims for Microsoft-manufactured hardware, like Surface and Hololens

- **Network Administrator** Can manage network locations and review enterprise network design insights for Microsoft 365 Software as a Service (SaaS) applications

- **Office Apps Administrator** Can manage Office apps cloud services, including policy and settings management and can manage the ability to select, unselect, and publish "what's new" feature content to users' devices

- **Organizational Messages Writer** Can write, publish, manage, and review organizational messages for end users through Microsoft product surfaces.

- **Password Administrator** Can reset passwords for nonadministrators and Password Administrators

- **Permissions Management Administrator** Can manage all aspects of Microsoft Entra Permissions Management

- **Power Platform Administrator** Can create and manage all aspects of Microsoft Dynamics 365, PowerApps, and Microsoft Flow

- **Printer Administrator** Can manage all aspects of printers and printer connectors

- **Printer Technician** Can register and unregister printers and update printer status

- **Privileged Authentication Administrator** Can access the view, set, and reset authentication method information for any user (admin or nonadmin)

- **Privileged Role Administrator** Can manage role assignments in Azure AD and all aspects of Privileged Identity Management

- **Reports Reader** Can read sign-in and audit reports

- **Search Administrator** Can create and manage all aspects of Microsoft Search settings

- **Search Editor** Can create and manage the editorial content, such as bookmarks, Q&As, locations, and floorplans

- **Security Administrator** Can read security information and reports and manage configuration in Azure AD and Office 365

- **Security Operator** Creates and manages security events

- **Security Reader** Can read security information and reports in Azure AD and Office 365

- **Service Support Administrator** Can read service health information and manage support tickets

- **SharePoint Administrator** Can manage all aspects of the SharePoint service

- **Skype for Business Administrator** Can manage all aspects of the Skype for Business product

- **Teams Administrator** Can manage the Microsoft Teams service
- **Teams Communications Administrator** Can manage calling and meetings features within the Microsoft Teams service
- **Teams Communications Support Engineer** Can troubleshoot communications issues with Teams using advanced tools
- **Teams Communications Support Specialist** Can troubleshoot communications issues with Teams using basic tools
- **Teams Devices Administrator** Can perform management-related tasks on Teams-certified devices
- **Tenant Creator** Can create new Microsoft Entra or Azure AD B2C tenants
- **Usage Summary Reports Reader** Can see only tenant-level aggregates in the Microsoft 365 Usage Analytics and Productivity Score
- **User Administrator** Can manage all aspects of users and groups, including resetting passwords for limited admins
- **Virtual Visits Administrator** Can manage and share Virtual Visits information and metrics from admin centers or the Virtual Visits app
- **Viva Goals Administrator** Can manage and configure all aspects of Microsoft Viva Goals
- **Viva Pulse Administrator** Can manage all settings for the Microsoft Viva Pulse app
- **Windows 365 Administrator** Can provision and manage all aspects of cloud PCs
- **Windows Update Deployment Administrator** Can create and manage all aspects of Windows Update deployments through the Windows Update for Business deployment service
- **Yammer Administrator** Can manage all aspects of the Yammer service

> **MORE INFO** **MICROSOFT ENTRA BUILT-IN ROLES**
>
> To learn more about each Microsoft Entra Role and least-privilege by task, see *https://aka.ms/SC900_ME-IDRoles* and *https://aka.ms/SC900_ME-IDLeastPrivByTask*, respectively

Skill 2.4: Describe the identity protection and governance capabilities of Microsoft Entra

This objective deals with advanced security features and governance. All the functionality in this section requires a Microsoft Entra P2 or Microsoft Entra ID Governance license. You will learn why governance is important from a security and productivity perspective and common scenarios where you can implement governance practices. You will also learn about privilege identity management and how it can greatly reduce the risk related to administrative accounts. You will also learn how risk extends to your cloud infrastructure for your user accounts, groups, and application identities and how you can find and reduce it. Finally, you will learn about identity protection, its risk signals, and how they can prompt users for MFA only when risk is detected.

This skill covers:

- Identity governance
- Entitlement management and access reviews
- Privileged Identity Management (PIM)
- Microsoft Entra Permission Management
- Microsoft Entra ID Protection

Describe what identity governance is

Identity governance ensures the right people have the right access to the right resources over the full lifecycle of their accounts. This helps increase the security of the organization as well as enable productivity. Walking through a few scenarios will make the need for identity governance clearer.

Let's say a new employee starts in the sales department at your company. What resources should they have access to? Who determines this access? Who approves this access? Who reviews this access on an ongoing basis? How long does this process take? Let's say the employee asks their manager for help. The manager might put a request in with the help desk. The help desk now must pick up this request and process it. The employee might need to be added to multiple groups, sites, and applications. All these changes must be processed. This takes time, and the new hire isn't productive until it happens. What if an application or SharePoint site was missed in the manager's or help desk's initial request? Now, another request needs to be sent and manually processed. All the while, the employee can't start their new job.

Later, this sales employee will be ready to take on some new challenges and switch to a job in engineering. A similar process as above takes place. However, as part of that request, nobody thinks to remove the previous access. Now, the employee has access to all the resources for engineering and sales. Should they? Are there regulatory rules that require some of this data to be separate? Even though the employee didn't access the resource, can that be proven to an auditor? What about ethical rules between these two different data sets?

This scenario also applies to administrator accounts where the damage can be even more drastic. Someone who was once a SharePoint administrator and who moves into a new role without having their old admin privileges removed might be able to see more information than they should be able to see in the environment.

This also applies to external guest users. For example, Contoso is partnering with another company on a secret new product they will launch together. Should everyone at the partner company be able to access the SharePoint site where the secret documents are stored? Who is the right person to decide who at the partner company should be able to access them? If this is a long-running project, do people who completed their task at the beginning still need access at the very end?

These problems described are not unique to Contoso. These problems are also not new to the industry. You might have heard it previously described as identity lifecycle management, access lifecycle management, or joiner/mover/leaver (JML) process. Microsoft Entra identity governance features such as lifecycle workflows, automatic provisioning to applications and resources in the cloud and on-premises, entitlement management and access reviews aim to help a company address these four questions:

- Which users should have access to which resources?
- What are those users doing with that access?
- Are there effective organizational controls for managing access?
- Can auditors verify that the controls are working?

This exam section just begins to scratch the surface of some of the rich functionality available to administrators to standardize and automate many common tasks. For example, the Lifecycle Workflows has the following prebuilt templates to aid in these common joiner/mover/leaver (JML) processes.

- Onboard prehire employee
- Onboard new employee
- Post-onboarding of an employee
- Real-time employee change
- Pre-offboarding of an employee
- Offboard an employee
- Post-offboarding of an employee

These can be customized to your organization's needs and are also extremely extensible using Logic Apps. When you dig into this area, you'll see that many of these Microsoft Entra identity governance features can be combined end to end.

Describe what entitlement management and access reviews are

Entitlement management resolves some of the previous challenges around identity and access management at scale using automation. It does this by automating access request workflows, access assignments, reviews, and handling the expiration of access, which reduces the risk of forgetting or overlooking these important but manual tasks. The **Identity Governance** page can be reached by clicking **Entitlement Management** (see Figure 2-22).

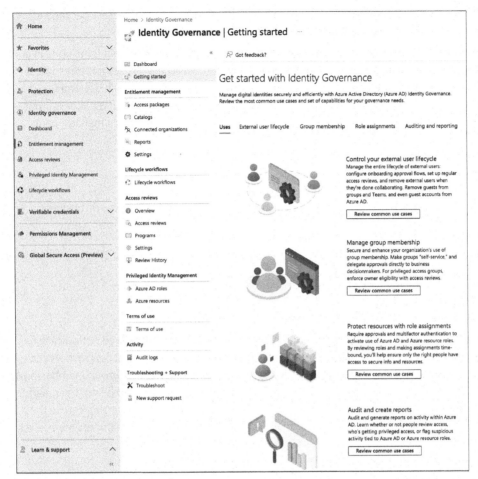

FIGURE 2-22 Identity Governance

Entitlement management uses access packages. An access package enables you to do a one-time setup of resources and policies that automatically administers access for the life of the access package. You can think of it as a bundle of resources a user would need to work on a project or perform a task. Access packages work well when departments want to manage their own access without IT involvement. For example, access packages are useful when access requires approval by individuals like a manager; employees need time-limited access for a particular task; or for external collaboration on a project with B2B guest users.

Using the Contoso example we've used throughout this chapter, instead of trying to ensure all members of the sales department have access to the correct resources every time a new person is added to the sales department or when a new sales resource needs to be assigned to all users, we can have an access package for the sales department. This would bundle all the resources anyone working in sales would need. This ensures that access is consistent for all sales department users; if a new resource needs to be added, it could be added to this one access package. This would also scale out for other departments in Contoso. We could have another access package for engineering. Likewise, we could also have an access package for our secret partner project that includes those Azure AD B2B guest accounts.

An administrator or a delegated access package manager can define what is included in an access package, meaning a business unit can manage its own access policies for its resources without IT involvement. Each access package has one or more policies, which determine who can request access, who approves requests, and the access expiration if the access is not renewed. The following are resources that can be managed with entitlement management:

- Membership of Microsoft Entra security groups
- Membership of Microsoft 365 Groups and Teams
- Membership to SharePoint Online sites
- Assignment to Microsoft Entra applications, which include SaaS or line-of-business (LOB) apps

> **MORE INFO** **MICROSOFT ENTRA ENTITLEMENT MANAGEMENT**
>
> To learn more about each Microsoft Entra entitlement management, see *https://aka.ms/ SC900_EntitlementMgmt.*

Another key aspect of governance is to make sure access is being reviewed periodically to ensure the people who no longer need access are removed. This is where access reviews can come into play. As shown in Figure 2-23, access reviews are used to review group memberships, access to applications, and role assignments. These reviews can and should be done regularly, such as weekly, monthly, quarterly, or annually. The reviewers of the membership can be the group owners or specified reviewers, or they can be self-reviewed by the members themselves.

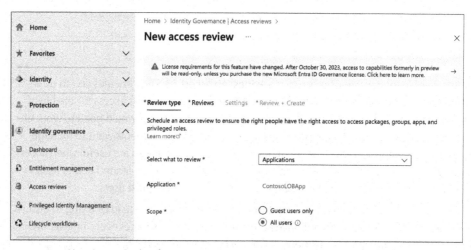

FIGURE 2-23 New Access Review for guest users

At the beginning of this section, we used a very common example in which an administrator changes roles, but their previous administrator permissions were not removed. This is one of the most important areas to focus on because of the power administrative access has in the environment. Periodically performing an access review to see who has been assigned to privileged roles is critical and is an excellent use case for access reviews.

Another important thing to consider regarding access reviews is who has access to business-critical data. Requiring users to self-review and justify why they still need access to this data is useful for auditing, especially for Microsoft Entra B2B guest accounts that might not be part of the regular IAM process.

Another excellent use of access reviews is the periodic review of users on an exception list for a company-wide policy. For example, let's say you've applied a Microsoft Entra conditional access policy to all business units in the environment to block legacy authentication. Further, let's say that some people who might not be able to comply with the policy have been granted an exception from the policy for a short period of time. Perhaps they were running an older version of Outlook and were getting an upgraded version in seven weeks. Someone would have to remember to remove them from this exception list in seven weeks. With access reviews, the exception list can be reviewed at regular intervals to ensure that users are not permanently exempt. If they need to continue to be exempt, a justification is provided. Again, this helps with the audit trail.

Access reviews should be used when automation isn't used for group membership or when the group is being reused for a new purpose. If there is no automation, the membership will get stale. Access reviews will help ensure only the correct people are in the group. When groups are used for purposes different from those originally intended, reviewing the membership is a good practice, and members should be removed based on this new purpose.

> **MORE INFO   ACCESS REVIEWS**
>
> To learn more about Access Reviews, see *https://aka.ms/SC900_AccessReviews*.

Describe the capabilities of PIM

Privileged Identity Management (PIM), as shown in Figure 2-24, allows you to remove standing admin access where accounts are permanent group members. PIM implements time-based and approval-based activation of administrative roles, which greatly reduces the exposure for the most privileged accounts in the environment.

For example, you could configure PIM so that help desk personnel only have the right to change a user's password for a maximum of 60 minutes once their request for that right has been approved by a specific authorized administrator. PIM differs from earlier administrative models where help desk personnel typically can change Microsoft Entra ID user passwords at any time, even when they don't need it. PIM enables you to do the following:

- Configure just-in-time privileged access to Microsoft Entra ID and Azure resources. Just-in-time access is limited to an amount of time (1 hour, 4 hours, 8 hours, and so on) rather than allowing permanent access to those resources.

- Assign time-bound access to resources using start and end dates. For example, if maintenance starts on Saturday and runs from 9 PM to 6 AM, this can be prescheduled, so the admin has elevated rights during this time.

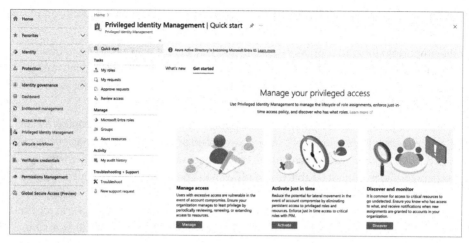

FIGURE 2-24 Privileged Identity Management

- Require approval from another administrator, user, or group when activating privileged roles.

- Require multifactor authentication to occur before role activation.

- Enforce Microsoft Entra Conditional Access policies to activate any role, such as coming from a compliant device or using a required authentication strength like a phishing-resistant credential.

- Require users to provide recorded written justification of why they must perform activation. This allows auditors at a later stage to correlate the administrative activity that occurs with the stated reason for providing privileged access.

- When privileged roles are activated, provide notifications, such as email alerts sent to a distribution list.

- Provide notifications when a privileged role is assigned outside of PIM.

- Perform access reviews to determine how often privileges are used and whether specific users still require roles.

- Export an audit history that internal or external auditors can examine.

Describe Microsoft Entra Permissions Management

Microsoft Entra Permissions Management is a cloud infrastructure entitlement management (CIEM)—prounouced *Kim*—product. Its main focus is to help organizations reduce risk by helping discover overpermissioned users, groups, and applications, such as service principals and serverless functions, and move to a least permissions model by removing excessive permissions. This is a key function of a cloud-native application protection platform (CNAPP) along with cloud security posture management (CSPM), cloud workload protection platform (CWPP), and multi-pipeline DevOps security.

Entra Permissions Management will first discover the permissions used by users, groups, and application identities and compare them to what permissions are assigned against the resources in Azure subscriptions, AWS accounts, and GCP projects. This difference in permissions assigned compared to permissions used is called the permissions gap. Many of these permissions are highly privileged for the environment.

For example, a user might be assigned the Owner rights on an Azure subscription. They can create, modify, and delete any resource in their environment. Entra Permissions Management evaluates the previous 90 days of usage and shows that this user only uses Azure permissions to create, start, and stop virtual machines.

This organization would have room to improve in its least-privilege strategy if this account were to make a mistake or be compromised; the damage it could do to the environment is vast. Entra Permissions Management calculates this aggregate score for users, groups, application identities such as service principals, managed identities, serverless functions, each Azure subscription, AWS account, and GCP project that is onboarded to Entra Permissions Management and calls it the Permissions Creep Index (PCI). This can be seen in Figure 2-25.

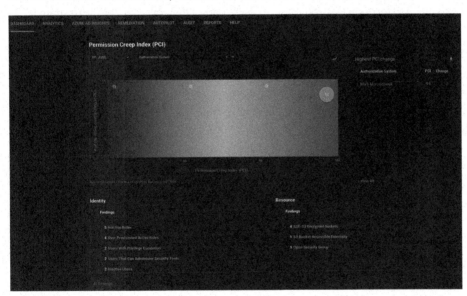

FIGURE 2-25 Entra Permissions Management

> **NOTE   CLOUDKNOX TO ENTRA PERMISSIONS MANAGEMENT UI TRANSITION**
>
> At the time of this writing, Entra Permissions Management is transitioning from the CloudKnox UI shown in Figure 2-25 to be more aligned with the look and feel of the Microsoft Entra admin center. This UI may look vastly different depending on when you read this chapter.

The second thing you'll do with Entra Permissions Management after discovery is look through the findings and reports to determine the biggest risk to our organization. There are various sets of prebuilt reports, like the Permissions Analytics Report, which helps guide you down the path of some of the most immediate things to resolve. This will highlight things such as accounts that essentially have administrative permissions, accounts that appear inactive and can be cleaned up, and some other critical configuration mistakes such as exposed ports or storage. You can also use the analytics pages to dig into this rich data set yourself to look for areas to reduce the permissions and the overall risk.

The next thing you'll do is remediate these overpermissioned resources. You can build roles in all three clouds based on the permissions used by a user, group, or application identity. You can also take this one step further for your human identities and leverage permissions on-demand, where a user can request a set of permissions or a role for a limited set of time. This can also follow an approval workflow where the request can be approved or denied.

Finally, we want to be able to monitor the permissions usage. Entra Permissions Management has a rich set of alerting capabilities. You can receive an alert the first time someone uses a high set of permissions they normally do not use or when someone is using permissions outside of their normal working hours. For example, much of the information in the Permission Analytics Report can also be alerted on when a new exposed storage is found. This is very helpful as customers continue to focus on least-privilege access as part of their broader Zero Trust strategy.

Describe Microsoft Entra ID Protection

Microsoft Entra ID Protection is Entra's advanced identity security capability. Identity Protection has three aspects: the console, the polices, and the risk events themselves.

The Identity Protection console shown in Figure 2-26 is used to investigate risk events. This provides an organizational view of the risky users, the number of users protected with risk policies, the mean time to remediate risk in the environment, attacks against the tenant aligned to the MITRE ATT&CK framework, and whether they've been blocked.

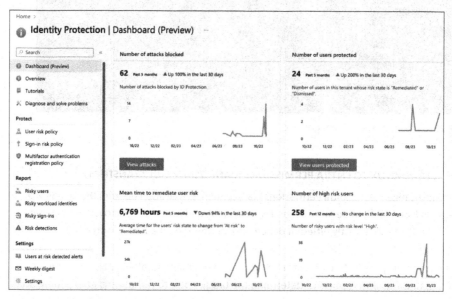

FIGURE 2-26 Identity Protection Overview

However, the real power is in the automating and remediation of identity-based risks through policies. These automation policies can be configured in Identity Protection or as part of a conditional access policy. There are two different types of policies:

- Sign-in risk policies represent the probability that the identity owner doesn't authorize a given authentication request. If a sign-in is determined to be risky, administrators can specify whether to block access or allow access but require multifactor authentication.

- User risk represents the probability that a given identity or account is compromised. It is the aggregate risk for the user. User risk policies allow administrators to block access, allow access, or allow access but require a password change with MFA when the policy is triggered.

Finally, there are the actual risk events themselves. There are two categories of risk events—user risk events that are calculated offline and sign-in risk events that are real-time and offline.

These user risk alerts include the following:

- **Leaked Credentials**   The user's clear-text username and password credentials have been discovered in a data breach either on the dark web or through other means.

- **Microsoft Entra Threat Intelligence**   The user activity that is unusual for the given user and is consistent with known attack patterns based on Microsoft's internal or external threat intelligence sources.

- **Possible Attempt To Access Primary Refresh Token (PRT)**   A PRT is a special type of JSON Web Token (JWT) that is used to enable single sign-in across applications. Attackers attempt to access this resource to move laterally in an environment or perform credential theft. This alert requires Microsoft Defender for Endpoint as the information is provided from the endpoint.

- **Anomalous User Activity**   This baselines normal user behavior and spots anomalous behavior patterns like suspicious changes to the directory.

- **User Reported Suspicious Activity**   This is reported when a user denies a multifactor authentication prompt and reports it as suspicious activity.

- **Additional Risk Detected**   This is reported when a tenant does not have a P2 license and activity occurs that is unusual for the user or consistent with known attack patterns.

These sign-in risk alerts include the following:

- **Anonymous IP Address**   When a user signs in from an anonymous IP address. While a user might use an anonymizing VPN to access organizational resources, attackers also use tools such as TOR nodes to launch compromise attempts.

- **Atypical Travel**   When a user's account sign-in indicates they have performed unusual shifts in their physical location, such as signing in from London and then from New Orleans in two hours. This is highly suspicious since a flight between the two cities takes much longer than two hours.

- **Anomalous Token**   This indicates the token has abnormal characteristics, such as an unusual token lifetime or it's being used from an unfamiliar location. This applies to both session tokens and refresh tokens.

- **Token Issuer Anomaly**   This indicates that the SAML token issuer for the associated SAML token is potentially compromised. The claims in the token are unusual or match known attacker patterns.

- **Suspicious Browser**   Indicates anomalous behavior based on suspicious sign-in activity across multiple tenants from different countries in the same browser.

- **Unfamiliar Sign-In Properties**   A user's sign-in properties differ substantially from those previously observed.

- **Admin-Confirmed Sser Compromise**   This indicates that an administrator has selected **Confirm User Compromised** through the portal or `riskyUsersAPI`.

- **Malicious IP Address**   sign-in from a malicious IP address based on high failure rates of invalid credentials or other IP reputation sources.

- **Password Spray**   When multiple usernames are attacked using a common password. This is triggered when a password spray has been performed.

- **Verified Threat Actor IP**   Indicates that sign-in activity is consistent with a known IP address associated with nation-state actors or cybercrime groups based on the Microsoft Threat Intelligence Center (MSTIC).

- **Microsoft Entra Threat Intelligence**   The user activity that is unusual for the given user and is consistent with known attack patterns based on Microsoft's internal or external threat intelligence sources.

- **Additional Risk Detected**   This is reported when a tenant does not have a P2 license and unusual activity occurs that might be consistent with known attack patterns.

- **Suspicious Inbox Manipulation Rules**   This comes from Microsoft Cloud App Security (MCAS) when suspicious rules that delete or move messages are set on the user's inbox.

- **Mass Access To Sensitive Files**   This comes from MCAS and is triggered when a user accesses multiple files from SharePoint or OneDrive. It will only trigger if the number of accessed files is uncommon for that user, and the files might contain sensitive information.

- **Impossible Travel**   This comes from MCAS when two user activities in a single or multiple session occur from geographically distant locations. Similar to the Atypical Travel event.

- **New Country**   This comes from MCAS and considers past activity locations to determine new and infrequent locations.

- **Activity From Anonymous IP Address**   This comes from MCAS and is similar to an anonymous IP address risk event.

- **Suspicious Inbox Forwarding**   This comes from MCAS and looks for suspicious email forwarding rules.

MORE INFO   **IDENTITY PROTECTION RISK GENERATION**

To generate your own identity protection risk events, see *https://aka.ms/ SC900_IdentityProtectionGenerateRisk.*

Thought experiment

In this thought experiment, demonstrate your skills and knowledge of the topics covered in this chapter. You can find answers to this thought experiment in the next section.

Identity and access at Contoso

You are one of the Microsoft Entra ID administrators for Contoso, an online general store specializing in various products for use around the home. As a part of your duties for Contoso, you have added a new SaaS application from the gallery in your Microsoft Entra tenant. Contoso cares greatly about the security of its environment. Contoso needs to ensure users are performing MFA or coming from a trusted device before accessing this new application. However, some users have access to trade secrets that should be accessed with the strongest form of credentials.

Contoso is also adopting and focusing on Zero Trust principles. Least privilege is a key focus for the administrator team, too. Today, admins have a separate permanent admin account to perform administrative actions. On further investigation, the amount of time the admin account is actually used is only a few hours a week. The admin account has these permissions 24 hours a day, 7 days a week, and 52 weeks a year. This is not following the principle of least privilege. Contoso must remove this permanent access and move to a model where administrators can use their administrative privileges when needed.

With this information in mind, answer the following questions:

1. How can you ensure users are signing in to resources from a corporate device or performing MFA?

2. What type of credentials should users accessing trade secrets use?

3. How can you ensure that administrators use their administrative access only when it is truly needed?

Thought experiment answers

This section contains the solution to the thought experiment.

1. You should configure a conditional access policy, and in the **Grant Controls** section, select **Require Multi-Factor Authentication**, **Require Microsoft Entra Hybrid**

Joined Device, and **Require Device To Be Marked As Compliant**. Then make sure **Require One Of The Selected Controls** is selected.

2. Phishing-resistant credentials such as Windows Hello For Business, FIDO2, or certificate-based authorization should be used and can be set in the conditional access policy scoped to those users and applied to that application in the **Grant Controls** section; select **Require Authentication Strength** and choose **Phishing Resistant MFA** from the dropdown.

3. You can configure Privileged Identity Management to remove all standing access. Administrators need to enable their privileged role when admin access is needed.

Chapter summary

- Microsoft Entra ID supports modern authentication protocols such as SAML, OAuth, and OpenID Connect and can also integrate with your on-premises apps using Microsoft Entra App Proxy.

- There are many different ways to authenticate to Microsoft Entra ID, such as password hash sync or pass-through authentication.

- Multifactor authentication has many methods available, and strong phishing-resistant methods should be a goal for all organizations.

- While passwords cannot be eliminated overnight, using Entra ID password protection can prevent users from entering weak and easily guessable passwords.

- Conditional access policies enable you to set the conditions for users, groups, and roles to access resources based on grant conditions.

- Microsoft Entra roles enable administrators to leverage RBAC and should follow least-privilege access whenever possible.

- Entitlement management helps ensure the right users have the right access at the right time, which can be proven with an audit trail.

- Privileged Identity Management enables just-in-time administration and just-in-time access to Azure resources.

- Identity Protection is the advanced identity security in Microsoft Entra ID that focuses on user and sign-in risk.

- Microsoft Entra Permissions Management helps organizations get to least privilege by highlighting users, groups, and applications that have permissions assigned they are not using and then moving them to a permissions set they need based on their usage.

CHAPTER 3

Capabilities of Microsoft security solutions

When designing a security solution using Microsoft technologies, it is important to consider the entire portfolio of options to have a complete approach for resources in Azure, Microsoft 365, and on-premises. These workloads must be equally monitored and protected and provide a seamless experience to the users. To manage active attacks, data from these workloads should be ingested into Microsoft Sentinel to ensure that you have a single view across your entire environment, which will facilitate the work of your security operations analysts.

To head off potential attacks, it's also important to focus on configuring and monitoring the security configuration of these workloads. To ensure that endpoint devices don't become the weakest link in your protection strategy, you need to leverage the security capabilities of Microsoft Defender for Endpoint.

Skills in this chapter:

- Skill 3.1: Basic security capabilities in Azure
- Skill 3.2: Security management capabilities in Azure
- Skill 3.3: Security capabilities in Microsoft Sentinel
- Skill 3.4: Threat protection with Microsoft 365 Defender

Skill 3.1: Basic security capabilities in Azure

It is important to understand the foundational security capabilities natively available in Azure. These capabilities will help you implement some of the Zero Trust principles covered in Chapter 1. This section covers the skills necessary to describe basic security capabilities in Azure according to the Exam SC-900 outline.

This skill covers how to:

- Identify DDoS protection capabilities using Azure DDoS protection
- Determine the use case to protect networks using Azure Firewall
- Protect web applications using Web Application Firewall
- Perform network segmentation using Azure virtual networks
- Determine the use case for Azure network security groups
- Identify scenarios that will benefit from the use of Azure Bastion
- Protect secret keys using Azure Key Vault

Azure DDoS protection

By default, Azure Distributed Denial of Service (DDoS) basic protection is already enabled on your subscription. This means that traffic monitoring and real-time mitigation of common network-level attacks are fully covered and provide the same level of defense as the ones utilized by Microsoft's online services.

While the basic protection provides automatic attack mitigations against DDoS, some capabilities are only provided by the DDoS Standard tier. What will determine which tier you will utilize is the organization's requirements. Contoso needs to implement DDoS protection on the application level in a scenario with real-time attack metrics and resource logs available to its team. Contoso also needs to create post-attack mitigation reports to present to upper management. These requirements can only be fulfilled by the DDoS Standard tier. Table 3-1 summarizes the capabilities of each tier:

TABLE 3-1 Azure DDoS Basic vs. Standard

Capability	DDos basic	DDoS standard
Active traffic monitoring and always-on detection	X	X
Automatic attack mitigation	X	X
Availability guarantee	Per Azure Region	Per Application
Mitigation policies	Tuned per Azure Region volume	Tuned for application traffic volume
Metrics and alerts	Not available	X
Mitigation flow logs	Not available	X
Mitigation policy customization	Not available	X
Support	Yes, but best effort approach	Yes, and provide access to DDoS experts during an active attack

Capability	DDos basic	DDoS standard
SLA	Azure region	Application guarantee and cost protection
Pricing	Free	Monthly usage

> **MORE INFO**   **ATTACKS COVERED BY DDOS**
>
> For more information about the different types of attacks that are covered by Azure DDoS, visit *http://aka.ms/sc900ddos*.

To configure Azure DDoS, your account must be a member of the **Network Contributor** role, or you can create a custom role that has read, write, and delete privileges under `Microsoft.Network/ddosProtectionPlans` and with action privileges under `Microsoft.Network/ddosProtectionPlans/join`. Your custom role also needs to have read, write, and delete privileges under `Microsoft.Network/virtualNetworks`.

Azure Firewall

While NSG provides stateful package flow and custom security rules, you will need a more robust solution to protect an entire virtual network. A company that needs a fully stateful, centralized network firewall-as-a-service (FwaaS), that provides network and application-level protection across different subscriptions and virtual networks should choose the Azure Firewall.

Azure Firewall can also span multiple availability zones for increased availability. Although there's no additional cost for an Azure Firewall deployed in an availability zone, there are additional costs for inbound and outbound data transfers associated with Availability Zones. Figure 3-3 shows some of the capabilities available in Azure Firewall.

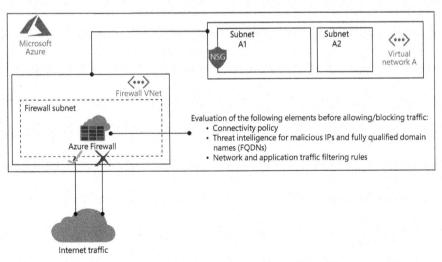

FIGURE 3-1 Azure Firewall topology

As shown in Figure 3-1, Azure Firewall will perform a series of evaluations before allowing or blocking the traffic. Just like in the NSG, the rules in Azure Firewall are processed according to the rule type in the priority order (lower numbers to higher numbers). A rule collection name can have only letters, numbers, underscores, periods, or hyphens.

You can configure NAT, network, and application rules on Azure Firewall. Remember that Azure Firewall uses a static public IP address for your virtual network resources, and you need that before deploying your Firewall. Azure Firewall also supports learning routes via the Border Gateway Protocol (BGP).

Azure Firewall will query the network and application rules to evaluate outbound traffic. Like in NSG, no other rules are processed when a match is found in a network rule. Azure Firewall will use the infrastructure rule collection if there is no match. This collection is created automatically by Azure Firewall and includes platform-specific fully qualified domain names (FQDN). If there is still no match, Azure Firewall denies outgoing traffic.

Azure Firewall uses rules based on Destination Network Address Translation (DNAT) for incoming traffic evaluation. These rules are also evaluated in priority, and they are evaluated before network rules. An implicit corresponding network rule is added to allow the translated traffic if a match is found. Although this is the default behavior, you can override this by explicitly adding a network rule collection with deny rules that match the translated traffic (if needed).

> **IMPORTANT** Application rules aren't applied for inbound connections. Microsoft recommends using Web Application Firewall (WAF) to filter inbound HTTPS traffic.

Figure 3-1 also shows that Azure Firewall leverages Microsoft Threat Intelligence during the traffic evaluation. The Microsoft Threat Intelligence is powered by Intelligent Security Graph and is used by many other services in Azure, including Microsoft Defender for Cloud.

Web Application Firewall

Web Application Firewall (WAF) provides centralized protection of your web applications from common exploits and vulnerabilities. Azure also allows you to deploy WAF in different manners, so it is important to understand the design requirements before suggesting which WAF deployment should be used.

Review the flowchart available at *http://aka.ms/wafdecisionflow* to better understand the available WAF options and how to select the best option according to your scenario. One of the reasons that lead you to use WAF with Front Door is when your scenario has all the following characteristics:

- It is a web application that uses HTTP/HTTPS.
- It is an Internet-facing app.
- It is globally distributed across different regions.
- The app is hosted in PaaS (such as Azure App Service).

Consider deploying WAF on Front Door when you need a global and centralized solution. When using WAF with Front Door, the web applications will be inspected for every incoming request delivered by Front Door at the network edge. If your deployment requires TLS offloading and package inspection, you can use WAF's native integration with Front Door, which allows you to inspect a request after it's decrypted.

If you need to protect your web applications from common threats such as SQL injection, cross-site scripting, and other web-based exploits, using Azure Web Application Firewall (WAF) on Azure Application Gateway is the most appropriate solution. WAF on Application Gateway is based on the Open Web Application Security Project (OWASP) core rule set 3.1, 3.0, or 2.2.9. These rules will protect your web apps against the top 10 OWASP vulnerabilities, which you can find at *https://owasp.org/www-project-top-ten*.

You can use WAF on Application Gateway to protect multiple web applications. A single instance of Application Gateway can host up to 40 websites protected by WAF. Even though you have multiple websites behind the WAF, you can still create custom policies to address the needs of those sites. See Figure 3-2.

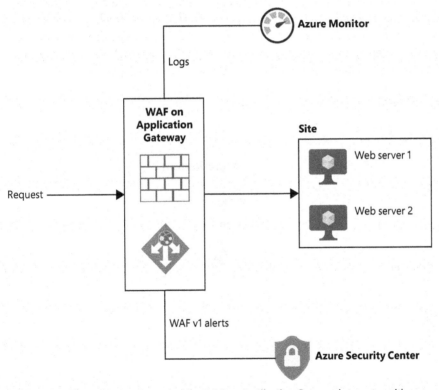

FIGURE 3-2 Different components that the WAF on Application Gateway integrates with

In Figure 3-2, a WAF policy is configured for the back-end site. This policy is where you define all rules, custom rules, exclusions, and other customizations, such as file upload limits.

WAF on Application Gateway supports Transport Layer Security (TLS) termination, cookie-based session affinity, round-robin load distribution, and content-based routing. The diagram shown in Figure 3-2 also highlights the integration with Azure Monitor, which will receive all logs related to potential attacks against your web applications. WAF v1 (version 1) alerts will also be streamed to Microsoft Defender for Cloud and appear in the Security Alert dashboard.

Network segmentation with Azure virtual networks

Network segmentation is the practice of separating resources for security or application of governance across workloads. Network segmentation also supports the Zero Trust model and applies security in a layered model as part of a defense-in-depth strategy.

To help contain an attacker if a breach occurs, workloads should be placed into separate network segments where you can control traffic to/from the segments. If one segment is compromised, you will be better able to contain the attack and prevent it from spreading laterally. If you don't segment your workloads, the attacker can spread laterally to all assets very easily.

An Azure virtual network (VNet) is the fundamental building block for a private network in Azure. Resources can be assigned to VNets to create segmentation and group-like resources in the VNet. Azure virtual networks can be created with multiples per region per subscription, and smaller subnets can be created within each VNet. No traffic can cross VNets by default and must specifically be provisioned. Figure 3-3 shows a simple form of multiple VNets.

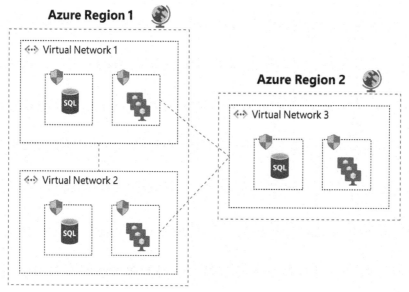

FIGURE 3-3 Azure VNets

Azure network security groups

Network security group (NSG) in Azure enables you to filter network traffic by creating rules that allow or deny inbound network traffic to or outbound network traffic from different types of resources. For example, you could configure an NSG to block traffic from the Internet inbound to a specific subnet, only allowing traffic that comes from a Network Virtual Appliance (NVA). Some organizations may use network segmentation and NSGs in a similar approach that VLANs (virtual local area networks) were utilized in on-premises infrastructure.

NSGs can be enabled on the subnet or to the network interface in the virtual machine (VM), as shown in Figure 3-4.

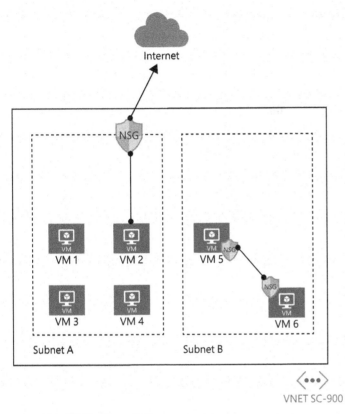

FIGURE 3-4 NSG implementations

In Figure 3-4, the NSG is assigned to Subnet A, which can be a good way to secure the entire subnet with a single set of NSG rules. However, you might need to control the NSG on the network interface level, shown in Subnet B, where VM 5 and VM 6 have an NSG assigned to the network interface.

When traffic is coming through the VNet (inbound traffic), Azure processes the NSG rules associated with the subnet first, if there is one, and then the NSG rules associated with the network interface. When the traffic leaves the VNet (outbound traffic), Azure processes the NSG rules associated with the network interface first, followed by the NSG rules associated with the subnet.

When you create an NSG, you need to configure a set of rules to harden the traffic. These rules have the following parameters:

- **Name** The name of the rule.
- **Priority** The order in which the rule will be processed. Lower numbers have high priority, meaning a rule priority 100 will be evaluated before a rule with a priority of 300. Once the traffic matches the rule, it will stop evaluating other rules. When configuring the priority, you can assign a number between 100 and 4096.
- **Source Ports** Defines the source IP, CIDR block, service tag, or application security group.
- **Destination** Defines the destination IP, CIDR block, service tag, or application security group.
- **Protocol** Defines the TCP/IP protocol that will be used, which can be **TCP**, **UDP**, **ICMP**, or **Any**.
- **Port Range** Define the port range or a single port.
- **Action** Can be configured to **Allow** or **Deny**.

Before creating a new NSG and adding new rules, it is important to know that Azure automatically creates default rules on an NSG deployment, as shown here:

- **Name** AllowVNetInBound
- **Priority** 6500
- **Source** VirtualNetwork
- **Source Ports** 0-65535
- **Destination** VirtualNetwork
- **Destination Ports** 0-65535
- **Protocol** Any
- **Access** Allow
- **Priority** 6501
- **Source** AzureLoadBalancer
- **Source Ports** 0-65535
- **Destination** 0.0.0.0/0
- **Destination Ports** 0-65535
- **Protocol** Any
- **Access** Allow
- **Name** DenyAllInbound
- **Priority** 6501
- **Source** AzureLoadBalancer
- **Source Ports** 0-65535
- **Destination** 0.0.0.0/0

- **Destination Ports** 0-65535
- **Protocol** Any
- **Access** Deny

Here is a list of outbound rules that are created by default:

- **Name** AllowVnetOutBound
- **Priority** 6501
- **Source** VirtualNetwork
- **Source Ports** 0-65535
- **Destination** VirtualNetwork
- **Destination Ports** 0-65535
- **Protocol** Any
- **Access** Allow
- **Priority** 6501
- **Source** 0.0.0.0/0
- **Source Ports** 0-65535
- **Destination** Internet
- **Destination Ports** 0-65535
- **Protocol** Any
- **Access** Allow
- **Priority** 6501
- **Source** 0.0.0.0/0
- **Source Ports** 0-65535
- **Destination** 0.0.0.0/0
- **Destination Ports** 0-65535
- **Protocol** Any
- **Access** Deny

> ***IMPORTANT*** Keep in mind that these default rules cannot be removed; if necessary, you can override them by creating rules with higher priorities.

Follow these steps to create and configure an NSG, which in this example will be associated with a subnet:

1. Navigate to the Azure portal by opening *https://portal.azure.com*.

2. In the search bar, type **network security**, and under **Services**, click **Network Security Groups**. The **Network Security Groups** page will appear.

3. Click the **Add** button; the **Create Network Security Group** page appears, as shown in Figure 3-5.

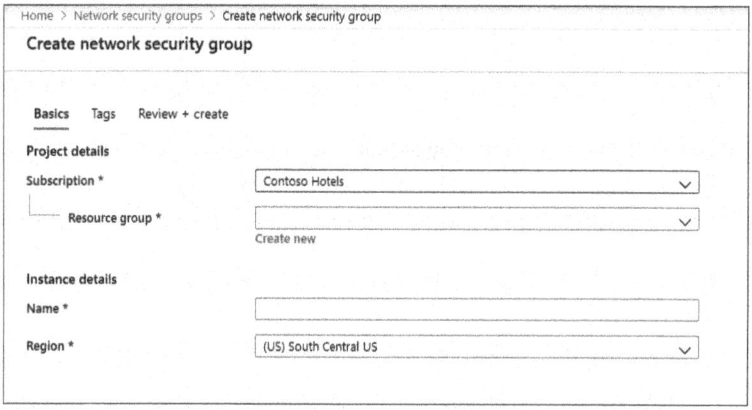

FIGURE 3-5 Initial parameters of the network security group

4. In the **Subscription** field, select the subscription where this NSG will reside.

5. In the **Resource group** field, select the resource group in which this NSG will reside.

6. In the **Name** field, type the name for this NSG.

7. In the **Region** field, select the Azure region in which this NSG will reside.

8. Click the **Review + Create** button, review the options, and click the **Create** button.

9. Once the deployment is complete, click the **Go To Resource** button; the NSG page appears.

At this point, you have successfully created your NSG, and you can see that the default rules are already part of it.

Azure Bastion

Azure Bastion is a PaaS service that you can deploy to connect to a virtual machine using your browser and the Azure portal. Azure Bastion can be leveraged to fulfill the least-access principles of Zero Trust by allowing you to implement just-in-time (JIT) access and just enough access (JEA).

Azure Bastion deployment is done per virtual network, which means you provision the Azure Bastion service in the VNet, and at that point, the RDP/SSH access will be available to all virtual machines that belong to the same VNet. The general architecture looks like Figure 3-6.

> **IMPORTANT** A session should be initiated only from the Azure portal. If you go directly to the URL from another browser session or tab, you may get a "Your session has expired" error message.

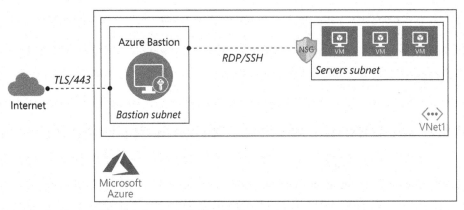

FIGURE 3-6 Core architecture for Azure Bastion deployment

Bastion is the best design choice if you don't want to use a public IP on the VMs but need to provide external RDP access to those VMs. Another advantage of not exposing the public IP (v4 only) address is that your VM will not receive port-scanning attacks.

Although Azure Bastion will receive external requests, you don't need to worry about hardening the service since Azure Bastion is a fully managed PaaS service, and the Azure platform keeps Azure Bastion hardened and up to date for you. This approach also helps to prevent zero-day exploits. Azure Bastion allows up to 25 concurrent RDP sessions and 50 concurrent SHC connections. Although this is the official limit, a high usage session may affect how Azure Bastion answers other connections, which means it can allow less than the maximum according to the conditions.

To establish a connection to Azure Bastion, you need the **Reader** role on the virtual machine, the **Reader** role on the NIC with the VM's private IP, and the **Reader** role on the Azure Bastion resource.

Azure Key Vault

Azure Key Vault allows you to store information that should not be made public, such as secrets, certificates, and keys. As Key Vaults can store sensitive information, you naturally want to limit who has access to it rather than allowing access to the whole world. You manage Key Vault access at the management and data planes. The management plane is the tools you use to manage Key Vault, such as the Azure portal, Azure CLI, and Cloud Shell. When you control access at the management plane, you can configure who can access the contents of the Key Vault at the data plane.

From the Key Vault perspective, the data plane involves the items stored in the Key Vault, and access permissions allow you to add, delete, and modify certificates, secrets, and keys. Access to the Key Vault at both the management and data planes should be as restricted as possible. If a user or application doesn't need access to the Key Vault, they shouldn't have access to it. Microsoft recommends using separate Key Vaults for development, preproduction, and production environments.

Each Key Vault you create is associated with the Azure AD tenancy linked to the subscription hosting the Key Vault. All attempts to manage or retrieve Key Vault content require Azure AD authentication. An advantage of requiring Azure AD authentication is that it allows you to determine which security principal is attempting access. Access to Key Vault cannot be granted based on having access to a secret or key and requires some form of Azure AD identity.

Skill 3.2: Security management capabilities in Azure

For your defense-in-depth strategy to succeed, you need visibility and control across different Azure workloads. Also, you must improve your security posture as you continue providing new resources. To accomplish that, you will leverage the capabilities available in Microsoft Defender for Cloud. This section covers the skills necessary to describe security management capabilities in Azure according to the Exam SC-900 outline.

> **This skill covers how to describe:**
> - The importance of cloud security posture management
> - The capabilities available in Microsoft Defender for Cloud
> - The enhanced security features of Microsoft Defender for Cloud
> - The usage of security baselines in Azure

Cloud security posture management

As enterprises start their journey to the cloud, they will face many challenges trying to adapt their on-premises tools to a cloud-based model. In a cloud computing environment, where there are different workloads to manage, it becomes imperative to have ongoing verification and corrective actions to ensure that the security posture of those workloads is always at the highest quality possible.

The adoption of a cloud security posture management (CSPM) platform helps organizations identify and remediate risks by leveraging this platform to provide visibility, uninterrupted monitoring, and remediation workflows to search for misconfigurations across diverse cloud environments and infrastructure, including cloud workloads and on-premises.

Defender for Cloud

Microsoft Defender for Cloud gives organizations complete visibility and control over the security of cloud workloads in Azure, on-premises, or another cloud provider. By actively monitoring these workloads, Defender for Cloud enhances the overall security posture of the cloud deployment and reduces the exposure of resources to threats. Defender for Cloud also uses intelligent threat detection to protect your environment from rapidly evolving cyberattacks.

Defender for Cloud also assesses the security of your hybrid cloud workload and provides recommendations to mitigate threats. In addition, it provides centralized policy management to ensure compliance with company or regulatory security requirements. Defender for Cloud has a variety of capabilities that can be used in two categories of cloud solutions:

- **Cloud Security Posture Management (CSPM)** Enable organizations to assess their cloud infrastructure to ensure compliance with industry regulations and identify security vulnerabilities in their cloud workloads.

- **Cloud Workload Protection (CWP)** Enable organizations to assess their cloud workload risks and detect threats against their servers (IaaS, on-premises, and in different cloud providers), containers, PaaS components such as databases (storage, KeyVault, AppServices, and APIs.

It is always recommended to start your cloud security journey by ensuring that you have visibility across all workloads, and once you have this visibility, you want to understand the security state of these workloads. With the CSPM foundational plan (which is free) available in Microsoft Defender for Cloud, you will be able to obtain foundational security hygiene information about your workloads located in Azure or other cloud providers such as Amazon Web Services (AWS) or Google Cloud Provider (GCP). Upon identifying these security recommendations, you can start working to remediate and improve your overall security posture.

After improving the security hygiene of the environment, you also want to be aware of potential threat actors trying to compromise your workloads, and that's where CWP capabilities will come into play. An important factor about threat detections tailored specifically for a particular workload is that you only monitor threats that are truly relevant to that workload. Microsoft Defender for Cloud has different plans that help protect various supported workloads.

Defender for Cloud also assesses the security of your hybrid cloud workloads, and it provides centralized policy management to ensure compliance with company or regulatory security requirements. Because Defender for Cloud is an Azure service, you must have an Azure subscription to use it—even if it's just a trial subscription. With an Azure subscription, you can activate the free Defender for Cloud CSPM tier, also known as Foundational CSPM. This free tier monitors compute, network, storage, and application resources in Azure. It also provides security policy, security assessment, security recommendations, and the ability to connect with other security partner solutions. Organizations starting with Infrastructure as a Service (IaaS) in Azure can benefit even from this free service because it will improve their security posture.

To access the Defender for Cloud dashboard, sign into the Azure portal (*https://portal.azure.com*) and click **Defender For Cloud** in the left pane. What happens the first time you open the Defender for Cloud dashboard may vary according to the type of workloads you have in your environment. For this example, the dashboard is fully populated with resources, recommendations, and alerts, as shown in Figure 3-7.

FIGURE 3-7 Defender for Cloud main dashboard

Defender for Cloud uses Role-Based Access Control (RBAC) based in Azure. By default, there are two roles in Defender for Cloud: **Security Reader** and **Security Admin**. The **Security Reader** role should be assigned to all users who only need read access to the dashboard. For example, security operations personnel who need to monitor and respond to security alerts should be assigned the **Security Reader** role.

Workload owners usually need to manage a particular cloud workload and its related resources. Besides that, the workload owner is responsible for implementing and maintaining protections in accordance with company security policy. Because of those requirements, assigning the Security Admin role for users with a workload would be appropriate. Only subscription **Owners**, **Contributors**, and **Security Admins** can edit a security policy. Only subscription and resource group **Owners** and **Contributors** can apply security recommendations for a resource.

Large organizations with different business units that are adopting Azure in a noncohesive way may find challenges when trying to adopt Defender for Cloud because they don't have visibility of all subscriptions that are part of their tenant. For this reason, even before enabling Defender for Cloud, you need to work with your IT team to identify all subscriptions that belong to the tenant and verify whether you have the right privileges to manage Defender for Cloud. In some scenarios, the same company may even have multiple tenants, with different subscriptions for each tenant.

When multiple subscriptions are part of the same tenant, and you need to centralize policy across subscriptions, you can use Azure Management Groups. By aggregating multiple subscriptions under the same management group, you can create one Role-Based Access Control (RBAC) assignment on the management group, which will inherit that access to all the subscriptions. This saves time on management because you can enable users to access everything they need instead of scripting RBAC across different subscriptions. Defender for Cloud also supports assigning security policies to a management group.

Defender for Cloud will identify resources needing security recommendations and automatically suggest changes. You can see all recommendations in a single place, which is available by choosing **General > Recommendations**; there, you can access the security controls shown in Figure 3-8 by expanding each security control to see the recommendations.

To see a list of all recommendations, set the **Group By Controls** option to **Off**. When planning your Defender for Cloud adoption, make sure to include a full revision of all recommendations even before exploring more capabilities. You can use the Defender for Cloud Secure Score impact to prioritize which security controls you should address first.

Name ↑↓	Max score ↓	Current score ↑↓	Potential score increase ↑↓	Status ↑↓	Unhealthy resources	Insights
> Enable MFA	10	10.00		● Completed	0 of 1 resources	
> Apply system updates	6	2.50	+ 12%	● Unassigned	7 of 12 resources	
> Encrypt data in transit	4	1.45	+ 9%	● Unassigned	7 of 11 resources	
> Manage access and permissions	4	0.00	+ 1%	● Unassigned	1 of 23 resources	
> Enable encryption at rest	4	0.00	+ 14%	● Unassigned	8 of 12 resources	
> Remediate security configurations	4	2.33	+ 6%	● Unassigned	5 of 12 resources	
> Restrict unauthorized network access	4	4.00		● Completed	0 of 14 resources	
> Apply adaptive application control	3	1.91	+ 4%	● Unassigned	4 of 11 resources	
> Enable endpoint protection	2	0.50	+ 5%	● Unassigned	9 of 12 resources	
> Enable auditing and logging	Not scored	Not scored		● Completed	0 of 2 resources	
> Enable enhanced security features	Not scored	Not scored		● Unassigned	2 of 2 resources	
> Implement security best practices	Not scored	Not scored		● Unassigned	3 of 37 resources	

FIGURE 3-8 Aggregation of all security controls that contain recommendations in Defender for Cloud

CSPM capabilities

Regarding what to prioritize during your cloud security strategy, security hygiene should be your top priority. Most attackers are still succeeding due to a lack of security hygiene. The features available in Defender for Cloud will give you the level of visibility you need to improve your security hygiene and enhance your security posture.

The Foundational CSPM plan enables you to have a series of recommendations to prioritize what needs to be remediated, and these security improvements will be reflected in your Azure Secure Score. Defender for Cloud reviews your security recommendations across all workloads, applies advanced algorithms to determine the criticality of each recommendation, and calculates your Secure Score based on them. This Secure Score is shown on the main **Overview** page on its own **Secure Score** tile, as shown in Figure 3-9.

The overall Secure Score shown in the main dashboard is an accumulation of all your recommendation scores. Keep in mind that this score can vary because it reflects the subscription that is currently selected and the resources that belong to that subscription. If you have multiple subscriptions selected, the calculation will be for all subscriptions. The active recommendations on the selected subscription also make this score change. Recommendations are aggregated in security *controls*, which impact the Secure Score. A Secure Score increase only happens if *all* recommendations within a security control that apply to a particular resource are remediated. The example shown in Figure 3-10 is from the **Enable MFA** security control.

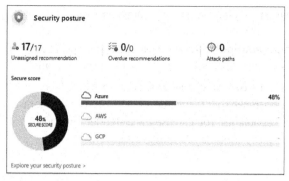

FIGURE 3-9 Secure Score tile

Name ↑↓	Max score ↓	Current score ↑↓	Potential score increase ↑↓	Status ↑↓	Unhealthy resources	Insights
∨ Enable MFA	10	10.00 ▮▮▮▮▮▮▮▮▮▮		✓ Completed	0 of 1 resources	
Accounts with owner permissions on Azure re...				✓ Completed	⚠ 0 of 1 subscription	
Accounts with write permissions on Azure res...				✓ Completed	⚠ 0 of 1 subscription	

FIGURE 3-10 Enable MFA security control

> **TIP** For detailed information on how the Secure Score is calculated, visit *http://aka.ms/sc900securescore.*

For organizations that need a more contextual approach to security posture management, the Defender CSPM plan is the recommended solution to be enabled. With Defender CSPM, you have more advanced capabilities to help prevent attacks and prioritize recommendations, considering risk factors such as the number of vulnerabilities, potential Internet exposure, and lateral movement. Table 3-2 shows a comparison between these two plans.

TABLE 3-2 CSPM plans comparison

Capability	Foundational CSPM	Defender CSPM
Security recommendations	X	X
Secure Score	X	X
Inventory	X	X
Security policy	X	X
Workflow automation	X	X
Data visualization and reporting with Azure Workbooks	X	X
Data exporting	X	X
Microsoft Cloud Security Benchmark	X	X

Capability	Foundational CSPM	Defender CSPM
Governance		X
Regulatory compliance		X
Cloud security explorer		X
Attack path analysis		X
Agentless scanning for machines		X
Agentless discovery for Kubernetes		X
Container registry vulnerability assessment, including registry scanning		X
Data-aware security posture		X
External Attack Surface Management (EASM) insights		X

How security policies and initiatives improve the cloud security posture

Defender for Cloud recommendations are based on the Microsoft Cloud Security Benchmark (MCSB) built-in definition in Azure Policy. MCSB was created with the idea of providing a canonical set of Azure-centric technical security controls based on controls defined by the Center for Internet Security (CIS), the National Institute of Standards and Technology (NIST), and the Payment Card Industry (PCI).

MCSB comprises security controls and a service baseline. A security control (also called compliance control) specifies a feature or activity that needs to be addressed but is not necessarily related to a technology or implementation. For example, network security is one of the security controls available in MCSB. It contains specific actions that must be addressed to help ensure that the network is more secure. A service baseline is basically the implementation of the control in individual Azure services. For example, an organization needs to improve its database security posture, and implementing an Azure SQL security baseline is one action that can be taken. Defender for Cloud leverages MCSB for its own set of security recommendations, which means that as you remediate security recommendations in Defender for Cloud, you are automatically improving your level of MCSB compliance.

The remediation of recommendations will positively impact the Secure Score, which can be used to track your security posture enhancement over time. When reviewing recommendations to remediate, use the top-down approach on the Recommendations page to prioritize the security controls that improve your Secure Score by adding more points.

Organizations that are not mature and don't enforce policies upon the creation of resources may see their Secure Score dropping when new workloads are provisioned. This can happen because security settings were not enforced via security policies, and the workload gets provisioned without using security best practices. To avoid potential drops in Secure Score, ensure that you are working closely with the Azure Governance team to include guardrails at the beginning of the pipeline to force workloads to be deployed securely by default. You can use Azure Policy to deny the creation of resources that are not secure.

Enhanced security features of Microsoft Defender for Cloud

In addition to CSPM capabilities, Defender for Cloud has threat detection options available as part of the Cloud Workload Protection (CWP) plans. Organizations can leverage these plans to assess their cloud workload risks and detect threats against them. To use the CWP capabilities, you must enable a specific Defender for Cloud plan corresponding to the workload you want to protect. The current plans available are

- Defender for Servers
- Defender for App Service
- Defender for Databases (includes support for Azure SQL databases, SQL Server on machines, Azure Cosmos DB, and open relational databases)
- Defender for Containers
- Defender for Key Vault
- Defender for Resource Manager
- Defender for APIs

These plans will provide tailored threat detection that will vary according to the threat landscape of the workload. For example, the threat landscape of an SQL database is not the same as an Azure Storage account, so the threat detection needs to be customized for that specific workload.

Defender for Cloud CWP plans use machine-learning technologies to evaluate all relevant events across the entire cloud fabric. By using this approach, it is possible to quickly identify threats that are extremely hard to identify using manual processes. Defender for Cloud uses the following analytics:

- **Integrated threat intelligence**   This leverages global threat intelligence from Microsoft to look for known bad actors.
- **Behavioral analytics**   This looks for known patterns and malicious behaviors—for example, a process executed in a suspicious manner, hidden malware, an exploitation attempt, or the execution of a malicious PowerShell script.
- **Anomaly detection**   This uses statistical profiling to build a historical baseline and triggers an alert based on deviations from this baseline.

> **TIP**   Read more about Defender for Cloud detection capabilities and other relevant scenarios at *https://aka.ms/ascdetections*.

Some plans, such as Defender for Servers, offer more than just threat detection. When you enable Defender for Servers, you will also have a series of enhanced security features available, which include

- **Network Map** This enables you to visualize your entire Azure network infrastructure, including potential communication paths and VMs exposed to the Internet, and provide improvement recommendations.

- **Just-in-time VM Access** This enables you to restrict access based on the time necessary to access VMs from the Internet because they need remote access using RDP or SSH protocols. If the end user just needs external access for two hours, there is no need to keep the VM exposed. You can use this feature to control the time window in which the VM will be exposed to the Internet.

- **Adaptive application controls** This capability uses machine learning to learn more about the application's behavior and create an allowed list of applications that can safely run on the VM.

- **File integrity monitoring** This helps to protect the integrity of your system and applications by continuously monitoring the behavior of your registry and configuration files.

- **Network security group (NSG) hardening** This capability uses machine learning to learn about network communication between resources and suggests applying an access control list to harden network traffic.

- **Vulnerability assessment** Identifies VMs that don't have a vulnerability assessment solution installed and recommends installing either Microsoft Threat Vulnerability Management (TVM) or Qualys.

Security baselines for Azure

Compliance controls require that standard security controls are measured via configuration baselines. Many organizations rely on industry-standard controls for security best practices to improve their security posture. Security baselines for Azure focus on cloud-centric control areas, where these controls are consistent with well-known security benchmarks, such as those described by the Center for Internet Security (CIS).

MCSB is Microsoft's security control framework that enables customers to meet their security control requirements in Azure. To provide a seamless experience, MCSB became the default initiative in Defender for Cloud, which means that to track the security status of your live environment, you just need to monitor the results via Defender for Cloud dashboard. You can even visualize the mapping using the Regulatory Compliance dashboard, as shown in Figure 3-11.

> **TIP** For more information about MCSB, visit *https://aka.ms/benchmarkdocs*.

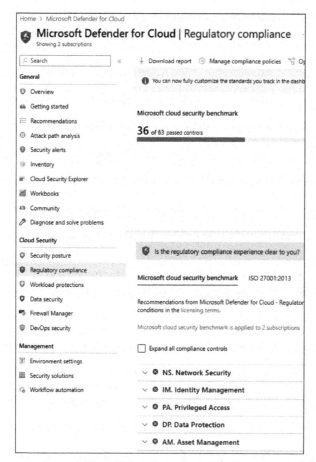

FIGURE 3-11 MCSB available in Defender for Cloud

While using MCSB will improve the security posture of your workloads in Azure, some scenarios might require you to use a different benchmark to measure compliance. This usually happens when an organization must comply with a certain standard based on the industry. For example, if the organization is part of the financial industry, it may need to comply with the Payment Card Industry (PCI) Data Security Standard (DSS).

You can leverage the same regulatory compliance dashboard in Defender for Cloud for scenarios where you need to monitor your Azure workloads based on an industry standard. Keep in mind that some controls will appear grayed out in the dashboard. This means these controls don't have any Defender for Cloud assessments associated with them, which could happen because some controls may be procedure- or process-related, and others don't have any automated policies or assessments implemented yet. When designing your security posture enhancement strategy based on industry standards, consider the standards supported by Azure that are reflected in Defender for Cloud.

Skill 3.3: Security capabilities in Microsoft Sentinel

This objective will cover the concepts of Security Information and Event Management (SIEM), Security Orchestration, Automation and Response, and Extended Detection and Response (XDR). These concepts are important to understanding threat protection and response in today's security information environment. The section will also cover Microsoft Sentinel and how it combines SIEM, SOAR, and XDR across the Microsoft Security stack.

This skill covers how to describe:

- Concepts of SIEM technology, including analytics, data aggregation, data correlation, data visualization, and data retention
- Concepts of SOAR and when to utilize
- How Microsoft Sentinel works and integrates with threat management

---

What is Security Information and Event Management (SIEM)?

Gartner defines an SIEM as technology that supports "threat detection and security incident response through the real-time collection and historical analysis of security events from a wide variety of event and contextual data sources."

Most traditional SIEMs started as on-premises solutions comprised of hardware and software that supported log ingestion and storage and provided a user interface and search engine to correlate system events and security alerts. As log ingestion and storage requirements increased, customers needed to buy larger hardware or distribute the workload across multiple servers. A SIEM usually provides the following capabilities to the SOC:

- Data ingestion/log aggregation
- Analytics
- Correlation
- Data visualization
- Data retention
- Forensic analysis

When analyzing a scenario on the SC-900 Exam, you must understand the organization's business requirements before recommending an SIEM solution. For example, Contoso must collect logs and analyze, correlate, and respond to security incidents across multiple security products and solutions, so an SIEM is needed. Extended detection and response products can do this for a specific area, such as an endpoint, but an SIEM can combine data and alerts across many security solutions.

Data and log aggregation

The core capability of any SIEM is to bring together data and logs from many platforms, such as network devices, application and system logs, and other security products. A SIEM allows organizations to collect logs from various sources and often allows them to be normalized into standard formats. Without this capability, organizations would need to jump from system to system, reviewing logs and trying to find security incidents that might have occurred.

The SIEM can collect logs from various sources using different methods. An agent can be installed on endpoints to collect and send logs locally. A collector can be deployed for systems where agents cannot be installed. For example, many network devices do not support having an agent installed, but they can send their logs out via SYSLOG, and then the logs can be collected. In today's cloud era, an SIEM should also provide ways to collect logs from SaaS (Software-as-a-Service) and PaaS (Platform-as-a-Service), where an agent cannot be installed on the source cloud service.

As data is collected, an SIEM can parse and normalize the data into standard formats to make it easy for the SOC to analyze or use it. Network devices from different vendors will have very different messages. While SYSLOG provides a basic message format, it is not comprehensive enough because organizations still need to parse the message field, which every vendor uses differently. ArcSight, a popular SIEM product from Micro Focus, created the Common Event Format (CEF), which has been adopted by many vendors and helped normalize device messages.

The format uses key-value pairs to allow vendors to match their logging data to a set of standard fields. It's made even more flexible because it allows vendors to add their own fields. Every SIEM on the market supports CEF as one of the standard formats. This is important because it allows the SOC to understand the data and fields when building analytics, visualizations, or hunting into the data.

> **MORE INFO   CEF**
>
> For more information about CEF, see *https://www.secef.net/wp-content/uploads/sites/10/2017/04/CommonEventFormatv23.pdf*.

Analytics

Once the SOC can collect data from environmental sources, analytics is the next most important capability in the SIEM. Analytics allow An SOC to discern anomalies from expected behavior and spot patterns that might be attacker activity.

Analytics allows the analyst to create a detection or rule that triggers based on specific parameters. For example, an analyst can easily spot 10 or more failed log-ins from a single user on a single machine, but it would be difficult for an analyst to see if those failed log-ins occurred across multiple systems over the course of 24 hours. To spot this behavior, an analyst could create a rule that creates an alert if ten or more failed log-ins by the same user occur across all systems. The analyst could then investigate these log-ins to determine whether the user had a legitimate issue or if an attacker was probing that user account.

While this is a basic example, many SIEMs today provide much more advanced analytics to analyze the data, create a normal pattern of failed log-ins, and alert on an anomalous failed log-in.

Correlation

Correlation allows events and/or alerts to be linked to incidents so the analyst can see the entire attack. Using the failed log-ins example from the previous section, let's say that we see 20 alerts for different users who have failed log-ins that met the criteria. In this case, we'd have up to 20 incidents to investigate. Correlation allows us to see that the source IP address was the same for all 20 of these failed log-ins, which allows the analyst to see that it is likely a single incident composed of multiple alerts. Correlation reduces the workload for the SOC analyst and allows them to see whether an attacker is trying to gain access to multiple accounts in the environment.

Data visualization

Today, all SIEMS can visualize data to allow the SOC to turn event data, alerts, and incidents into visual informational charts that help further understand the data. For example, the SOC could create or use a built-in visualization to see the key measures of the SOC, such as how many alerts occurred per day over the last month, the mean time to acknowledge incidents for the SOC, mean time to recovery (MTTR) for the analysts or the SOC, and the number of incidents assigned to each analyst.

The visualization can help the SOC manager determine if the SOC is performing as expected. The SOC can use visualization to see if any patterns are found in a single data source. For example, an analyst could look at Microsoft Entra sign-in logs to see daily trends, whether a spike or drop has occurred, or identify the top five types of log-ins (user, noninteractive, and so on).

Data retention

An SIEM must provide data retention for events, alerts, and incidents. Many organizations have industry or government compliance requirements to retain all or some subset of logs for a period of time. The SIEM either needs to store the logs directly or provide a way to export the logs to archived storage. Retention is also required for investigation and hunting. For example, let's say an attacker gains access to a system, and the system is reaching out to a command-and-control server on the Internet. If the SIEM only had logs for the past few days, the SOC analyst could not go back in time to see if any other systems have reached out to that same server IP address. The analyst couldn't tell if this was a one-time attack or if the attack had also occurred previously. Additionally, as other organizations discover attackers and share indicators of compromise (IoC) on those attacks, your SOC will need past data to determine whether the same attackers got into your environment without being detected.

All SIEMs can store and retain data for long periods, but this comes at a cost. Hot storage—which is needed for fast searching of the data—is much more expensive than cold storage. Some SIEMs provide the capability to interact with cheaper storage for data that is stored over a long term. Because of the cost, most SOCs retain 90 to 180 days in the SIEM and offload long-term data to other cheaper storage systems.

Forensic analysis

The investigation example in the previous section illustrates what is meant by "forensic analysis." The analyst can use the logs from many systems to investigate an incident to understand the full impact of the attack. This is a reactive type of analysis, meaning the analyst reacts to the incident and conducts forensics to determine what happened. An SIEM can also provide proactive analysis. SOC analysts could perform proactive hunting across the data sets to look for security issues for which the SOC might not have a detection.

For example, it would be interesting to proactively look at the top uncommon processes running on systems in the environment. The SOC wouldn't have detection for these processes because they don't know what process names to look for. By conducting proactive analysis (hunting), they could see the top five uncommon processes and discover an unknown or malicious process. They could then turn this into a security incident, conduct an investigation, and respond. If needed, the analyst could create a new analytic to detect whether that process is executed again, assuming it's bad.

What is security orchestration, automation, and response?

Security orchestration, automation, and response (SOAR) enables organizations to automate incident response and coordination detection and remediation actions across disparate systems. In the past, when a security incident was raised, an analyst would need to manually follow a response Playbook. The Playbook could be as simple as "reset the user's password," or it could be a more complex multistep operation. SOAR allows the SOC to automate these actions, reducing the workload on the analyst and creating a faster response time. In today's cybersecurity environment, minutes matter. Incidents occur more quickly, leaving less time for security analysts to manually triage, investigate, and remediate attacks.

Security orchestration allows the integration of these disparate systems through either built-in integrations or by allowing the use of application programming interfaces (APIs). The SOC might want to connect with many systems, such as threat intelligence platforms, vulnerability management systems, firewalls, and so on. Other non-security-related systems or APIs might need to be accessed, such as Azure itself.

Security Automation allows the SOC to automate typical security actions in response to incidents. Let's use the failed log-ins example provided earlier. The analyst might start by reviewing the failed log-in logs, extracting the source IP address, and then determining that IP address. Does it belong to the organization? If it was external, where did it come from? What country? Did I expect the user to log in from this location? These are time-consuming questions. To see where the user normally resides, the analyst must answer each of these questions from various systems, such as IP address management, the geolocation service, and

Azure Active Directory. Security automation allows the SOC to build Playbooks to automate these activities. The Playbook could query the IPAM system to see if it's a known address. An if statement or condition could then take the next action if the IP address is not a corporate IP. The Playbook could update the incident based on the results or even take actions, such as resetting the user's password and notifying their manager. Playbooks can be simple or very complex, and they can even call each other.

Security Response allows the SOC to review and monitor these automations. If a Playbook is automatically called during incident creation, the SOC might need to check the Playbook's status or review the Playbook's result later.

In the context of the SC-900 exam, you need to understand the business requirements that will lead you to recommend a SOAR solution. First and foremost, the organization must automate actions in response to security incidents. It must allow multiple systems to be connected via various methods, and it should allow response actions to be managed or monitored. It should also reduce the time the SOC takes to handle an incident.

Microsoft Sentinel

Over the last several years, more and more vendors have retooled their SIEMs to make them available in a Software as a Service or SaaS model. However, these SIEMS are typically built on top of a public cloud provider's infrastructure and don't offer the same benefits as Microsoft Sentinel regarding automatic scaling and storage. With Microsoft Sentinel, there are no requirements for the customer to open support tickets to scale out their service like other SaaS-based SIEMs. Microsoft handles all this automatically, and the customer can focus on the main task at hand, identifying and responding to cyberthreats.

Microsoft Sentinel is the world's first cloud-native SIEM and SOAR solution. It was built from the ground up in the cloud and allows organizations to scale with their SIEM and SOAR demands. Organizations can connect data across all users, devices, applications, and infrastructure. Data sources such as Microsoft Defender (an XDR solution) and third-party sources such as firewalls can be brought together to detect threats across their environments, both on-premises and across clouds. Organizations can use all this data to detect threats not previously detected by combining analytics and threat intelligence. Microsoft Cloud brings machine learning (a subset of artificial intelligence) to Microsoft Sentinel to detect and investigate security incidents. The SOC can search the data at scale, looking for anomalous activity. Microsoft Sentinel is integrated with Azure Logic Apps to provide SOAR capabilities to speed up security incident response and reduce the required time to incident resolution.

As discussed earlier, an SIEM must provide data and log aggregation. When this book was written, Microsoft Sentinel provided 103 data connectors. Data connectors are consistently being added, so this number will change over time. Figure 3-12 shows an overview of the **Data Connectors** blade in Microsoft Sentinel.

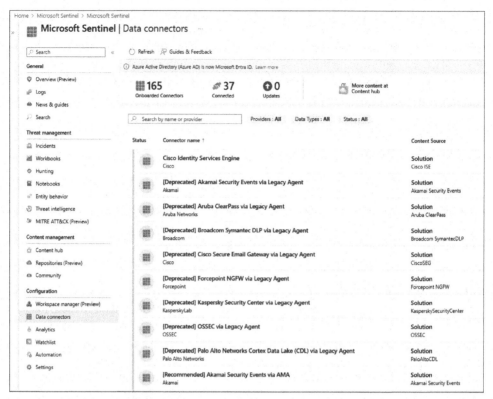

FIGURE 3-12 Data connectors page in Microsoft Sentinel dashboard

Microsoft Sentinel provides data connectors for Microsoft 365 Defender, Microsoft 365 sources like Office 365, many Azure services and diagnostic logs, and built-in connectors to a broader security ecosystem for non-Microsoft solutions. Also, several generic connectors exist for the Common Event Format, Syslog, and REST API to connect any data source in the organization's environment.

Many connectors are service-to-service, meaning Microsoft Sentinel connects directly to the cloud service. For example, each Microsoft 365 Defender product has a connector that brings security alerts from these products into Microsoft Sentinel. Office 365 and Dynamics 365 connectors are other examples of service-to-service connectors.

Other connectors use agents to collect logs from endpoints. Currently, Microsoft Sentinel uses the Log Analytics agent, which supports both Windows and Linux and can connect Windows Events, SYSLOG, and other log files on the endpoint.

> **TIP** The Log Analytics Agent is being replaced by the Azure Monitor Agent. You can find more information about this migration at *https://learn.microsoft.com/en-us/azure/sentinel/ama-migrate*.

Some connectors that don't have a service-to-service or agent collection method are also available. Typically, these use an Azure function to query data from other services and send the data to Log Analytics via a REST API.

How Microsoft Sentinel provides integrated threat management

When the WannaCrypt ransomware outbreak happened in 2017, security researchers were able to investigate how that worm exploited the vulnerability CVE-2017-0145, and they discovered a series of patterns used by this worm. They could identify how it changed the target system by reverse engineering the worm's behavior. Based on those artifacts, they were able to establish a list of those changes and document them as indicators of compromise (IOC). This list includes changes in the registry and the file system.

The use of analytics can be extremely beneficial for creating custom alerts that will trigger indicators of compromise that are found in the systems. This is a powerful way to identify compromised systems without warning from other security controls (such as antimalware that relies on signatures). While this is considered a reactive work, because the system was already compromised, you can also use analytics to identify whether a system is under attack. You can create alerts that use indicators of attack (IOA). By using analytics to create alerts based on an IOA, you can identify a potential attack in execution; for example, you can identify an attempt to elevate privileges to execute a built-in Windows tool, such as PowerShell, to download a piece of malware from a compromised site.

Also, using analytics can be useful to trigger alerts based on known malicious actors' techniques. For example, WannaCry used the attrib tool to perform file permission modification. You can investigate more details about the use of attrib and create alerts based on custom queries that will trigger once that technique is used.

An analytic rule can correlate events and security alerts into incidents. An incident is a discrete set of potential attacker activity represented by groups of related alerts that the SOC will need to triage. There are six analytic rule types:

- **Anomaly** Anomaly rules are built-in rules that use machine learning (ML) against your data to detect specific types of threats. These rules have a few parameters and thresholds that can be configured, but the ML models used are protected by Microsoft. You can enable these rules in flighting mode first to see how they would perform against your data, and when ready, you can move them to production.

- **Fusion** Uses Microsoft proprietary ML technology to automatically detect multistage attacks by combining several anomalous behaviors or suspicious activities that are part of the same attack kill chain.

TIP **ATTACK DETECTION SCENARIOS**

The Microsoft Sentinel documentation contains a list of attack detection scenarios for the Fusion rule type. See the documentation at *https://docs.microsoft.com/en-us/azure/sentinel/fusion*.

- **Machine Learning (ML) Behavior Analytics** Uses Microsoft proprietary ML algorithms to detect anomalous activity. Currently, there are two of these rule templates—one to detect anomalous Secure Shell (SSH) log-ins and another for Remote Desktop Protocol (RDP) log-ins.

- **Microsoft Security** In Microsoft Sentinel, analytic rules for Microsoft solutions are easy to create. This allows you to create an incident in Microsoft Sentinel from any existing security alert that comes from these solutions. You will not need to create individual analytic rules for Microsoft solution alerts. These rule templates will create an incident whenever an alert is generated by the source Microsoft solutions.

- **Scheduled** Scheduled analytics are your typical SIEM rule that runs on a schedule, looking at data from a specific time period. These rules trigger on a configured threshold.

- **Threat Intelligence** These rules match threat intelligence–related data from the threat intelligence database against the Common Event Format (CEF), DNS, and Syslog data. You don't need to write scheduled rules to match TI against these data sources; just enabling this rule will do all the matching for you.

An SOC should start by using rule templates to cover detection use cases they want to protect or monitor for in their environment. Rule templates are out-of-the-box detections that can be used to detect attacks in various data sources. If a template does not exist for the use case, there are also other samples in the Microsoft Sentinel Community. The Microsoft Sentinel Community is a GitHub repository of additional samples that SOCs can use with Microsoft Sentinel.

> **NOTE** **MICROSOFT SENTINEL COMMUNITY**
>
> The Microsoft Sentinel Community can be found at *https://github.com/Azure/Azure-Sentinel* or via the **Community** blade in Microsoft Sentinel.

INVESTIGATION CAPABILITIES

Once an analyst triggers a detection and creates an incident, the SOC must investigate it. Microsoft Sentinel provides a rich investigation experience so the SOC can quickly triage and respond to the incident.

Microsoft Sentinel provides two other capabilities for investigation: User and Entity Behavior Analytics (UEBA) and Hunting. UEBA analyzes incoming log sources and builds baseline behavioral profiles for entities. When investigating an incident, it is sometimes necessary to pivot to an entity, such as a user, to gain further insights into what has occurred with that entity. UEBA also uses various types of machine learning to gain insights for each entity, such as if it's the first time the user has ever accessed a server.

UEBA can give the analyst a better understanding of the entities involved in an incident. This will enable analysts to understand how far the attack may have gotten inside the environment beyond just what was found in the incident.

Hunting is a form of proactive investigation. It allows the SOC to hunt through the data to look for security threats that aren't triggering alerts yet. For example, you can't create an alert for a malicious process name if you don't know the process name. With Sentinel, the analyst can find uncommon processes across all the data, and if there is something malicious, create an incident for triage and build an analytic rule to detect it. The advantage of using this approach is that if the same events happen again, you have a rule and know the name.

Hunting provides one last capability—Livestream—to help the SOC. Livestream allows the analyst to run a query in real time and see any results as they come in. This can be used when the SOC has an indicator of compromise (IoC) they want to watch during an active incident. We will not cover the details of Livestream here.

THREAT RESPONSE WITH AUTOMATION

Automation rules provide a way to trigger automatic responses to security incidents. Automation rules can set the incident status and severity, assign an owner, apply a tag, or run a Playbook. Playbooks are collections of steps or workflow that can be run in response to an incident. Playbooks are based on Azure Logic Apps, which provides many connectors to various services for integration into the workflow.

> **MORE INFO   AUTOMATED RESPONSE**
>
> Some Playbook samples can be found at *https://github.com/Azure/Azure-Sentinel/tree/master/Playbooks*.

DATA VISUALIZATION

Once the SOC has ingested data into Microsoft Sentinel, it can be visualized and monitored using workbooks. Workbooks can be used with many of the provided templates, or you can create custom dashboards or modify an existing template to meet the organization's needs. When creating workbooks, you will also use Kusto Query Languange, which enables you to do advanced analytic searches using a structural query language.

Skill 3.4: Threat protection with Microsoft 365 Defender

This objective will cover the concepts of threat protection with Microsoft 365 Defender. Microsoft 365 Defender is a unified pre- and post-breach enterprise defense suite that includes both XDR and SOAR capabilities for detection and response, though it also includes preventive controls.

This skill covers how to describe:

- The components and general considerations for using Microsoft 365 services
- The components and use case scenarios for Microsoft Defender for Endpoint
- What are the benefits of using Microsoft Defender for Cloud Apps as a Cloud Access Security Broker (CASB) solution
- The use case scenarios Microsoft Defender for Identity can be used to protect your directory services
- How Microsoft Defender Vulnerability Management can be used to reduce vulnerabilities in the environment
- How to use Microsoft Threat Intelligence to enhance your security posture and overall threat defense
- The components of the Microsoft 365 portal

Microsoft 365 Defender services

Microsoft 365 (M365) Defender protects endpoints, email, identities, and cloud applications. Each product in the suite will be covered in the following sections. It's important to understand that each product is designed to work together to provide full threat protection across resource types in the environment. Microsoft 365 Defender provides the following unified capabilities:

- **Single pane of glass**   You can view all detections, assets, actions, and related information in a single incident queue at *security.microsoft.com*.
- **Combined incidents**   Alerts generated by each product are correlated and combined into a single incident and timeline analysis. This allows you to see the full attack scope and affected assets in one view (including additional context, such as the sensitivity of data affected by an incident).
- **Automatic response**   Critical information is shared between the products to allow for real-time response to help stop the progression of an attack. For example, Defender for Endpoint finds a malicious file. In this case, Defender for Endpoint can instruct Defender for Office 365 to scan and remove the file from all email messages.
- **Cross-product SOAR**   Automated investigation and response (AutoIR) helps automatically investigate and remediate attacks.
- **Cross-product threat hunting**   SOC teams can leverage raw data from each product to hunt for signs of compromise and create queries that can be used for custom alerting.

EXAM TIP

For the SC-900 exam, it is important to understand which products are part of the Microsoft 365 Defender suite and what capabilities are provided.

Microsoft Defender for Office 365

Microsoft Defender for Office 365 (MSDO) provides threat protection for inbound messages (email, other office files), links (URLs), and attachments for collaboration tools, including Microsoft Teams, SharePoint Online, OneDrive for Business, and Exchange Online. MSDO includes

- **Threat protection policies**   Configure policies to protect the organization
- **Reports**   View reporting to monitor MSDO
- **Threat investigation and response**   Prevent, investigate, respond, and simulate attacks
- **Automatic investigation and response**   Save time by automatically mitigating threats

MSDO Policies are configured to determine predefined threats' behavior and protection level. Policies can be configured for fine-grained threat protection at the user, organization, recipient, and domain levels. Policies can be configured for the following areas:

- **Safe Attachments**   Check email messages to provide zero-day protection. All messages and attachments that do not have a virus/malware signature are routed to a special sandbox that uses machine learning (ML) to detect malicious intent. If no suspicious activity is found, the message is delivered.
- **Safe Links**   Makes a time-of-click check to ensure the URL is safe. Malicious links are blocked, while safe links remain accessible.
- **Safe Attachments for SharePoint, OneDrive, and Microsoft Teams**   Like safe attachments, but scans files shared via collaboration software to protect the organization.
- **Anti-phishing**   Detects attempts to impersonate users and internal/custom domains and uses ML and advanced impersonation detection algorithms.

Figure 3-13 shows the Microsoft 365 Defender portal. The figure shows that MSDO policies can be configured by clicking **Policies & Rules** in the left menu under **Email & Collaboration**.

Reports provide real-time insights the SOC can use to understand the threats it faces with MSDO. MSDO provides a threat explorer dashboard, a threat protection status report, a file types report, and a message disposition report.

Organizations can use threat investigation and response to anticipate and understand malicious attacks. Threat trackers provide the latest intelligence from Microsoft on cybersecurity issues. The SOC can see the latest malware and recommendations to take action before the attack hits. Threat Explorer provides a real-time report that the SOC can use to analyze recent threats. Lastly, the SOC can use Attack Simulator to run realistic attacks on the organization to identify vulnerabilities.

Recently, MSDO added automated investigation and response (AIR) capabilities. This set of security Playbooks can run automatically when an alert is triggered or when the SOC manually runs it. The prebuilt Playbooks provide the SOC team with time-saving steps to investigate and mitigate threats.

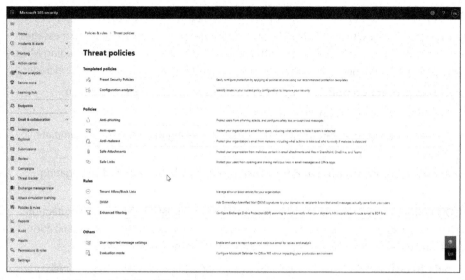

FIGURE 3-13 Defender for Office 365 policies

Microsoft Defender for Endpoint

Microsoft Defender for Endpoint (MSDE) protects endpoints, allowing enterprises to prevent, detect, investigate, and respond to advanced threats. For the SC-900 exam, it's important to understand the following MSDE areas:

- Threat and vulnerability management
- Attack-surface reduction
- Next-generation protection
- Endpoint detection and response
- Automated investigation and remediation
- Microsoft Secure Score for Devices
- Management and APIs

Threat and vulnerability management (TVM) provides the capability to discover, prioritize, and remediate endpoint vulnerabilities and misconfigurations. TVM uses the same MSDE sensor, so there is no need for an additional agent. It provides real-time device inventory, visibility into software and vulnerabilities, application runtime context, and configuration posture. TVM bridges the gap between security administrators and IT admins by integrating with Microsoft Endpoint Manager. Let's review the TVM dashboard:

1. Open a browser, visit *security.microsoft.com*, and sign in with a user who has **Security Administrator** privileges.

2. Click **Vulnerability Management** in the left menu and then select **Dashboard**. The **MSDE TVM Dashboard** appears, as shown in Figure 3-14.

3. Here, you can see an overview of threats and vulnerabilities.

- The Exposure Score for the organization is calculated from discovered weaknesses, the likelihood of a breach, and the device's value.

- In the center section, you can see the top recommendations list and the top events.

- On the right is the Microsoft Secure Score for devices.

- Scroll down to see exposure distribution by severity, remediation activities, top vulnerable software, and top exposed devices.

4. You can dive into each area for more information and to better understand your organization's risks and vulnerabilities.

FIGURE 3-14 Defender for Endpoint Threat and Vulnerability Management Dashboard

Attack surface reduction provides the capability to enable features in operating systems to reduce their attack surface.

- **Hardware-based isolation**   You can enable hardware-based isolation to ensure the system's integrity as it starts and while it's running.

- **Application control**   Application control can limit which applications are allowed to run to reduce the risk of rogue applications.

- **Controlled folder access**   Controlled folder access allows only trusted apps to make changes to controlled folders. This can prevent attacks like ransomware from changing controlled folders and files.

- **Network protection**   Network protection blocks outbound HTTP(S) traffic that attempts to connect to low-reputation sources (based on the domain name).

- **Exploit protection**   Exploit protection provides exploit mitigation techniques to operating system processes and apps.

- **Device control**   Lastly, device control allows you to protect against data loss by monitoring and controlling media used on devices.

All the capabilities in ASR can significantly reduce the chances of attack if they are enabled across the organization's devices.

MSDE is directly integrated with Microsoft Defender for Antivirus to provide next-generation protection on the endpoints. The protection provides machine learning, big data analysis, threat resistance research, and the Microsoft cloud to protect devices from new and emerging threats. Microsoft Defender for Antivirus is built into Windows 10 and Windows Server 2016+. It provides real-time antivirus with always-on scanning that uses file and process behavior monitoring. It can also detect and block apps that are deemed unsafe but might not be detected as malware. It provides cloud-delivered protection, which means it can detect and block emerging threats near-instantly by leveraging the Microsoft cloud.

Endpoint detection and response are the core components that make MSDE so powerful for SOCs. It continually collects behavioral cybertelemetry, including process information, network activities, deep optics into the kernel and memory manager, user log-ins, registry and file changes, so on. The information is stored in the cloud for six months, which allows analysts to view it back to the start of an attack. Once an attack is detected, a security alert is triggered. MSDE combines multiple alerts that are part of the same attack into incidents. This allows the SOC to see a full view of the attack. Let's take a look at the incident queue by following these steps:

1. Open a browser, visit *security.microsoft.com*, and sign in as a user who has **Security Administrator** privileges.

2. Expand **Incidents & Alerts** in the left menu and select **Incidents**.

3. Figure 3-15 shows the **MSDE Incidents** queue. Here, you can see the timeline chart of incidents over time, which might show a spike when increased attacks occur. Below the chart in Figure 3-15 is a list of open incidents. You can see the **Incident Name**, **Severity**, **Investigation State**, and more detailed information. The top of the list is the most important to investigate first.

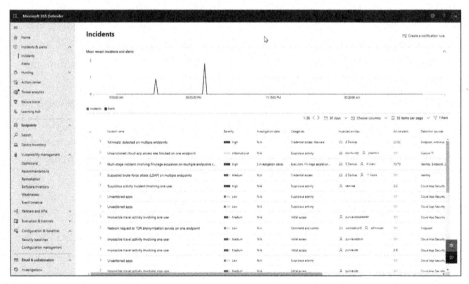

FIGURE 3-15 Incidents queue

4. Click an incident. Figure 3-16 shows the details of the incident. You can see an overview of everything involved in the incident, such as a timeline of security alerts, entities involved, and incident information. Near the top are tabs that allow you to dive deeper into each area to further investigate and respond to the attack.

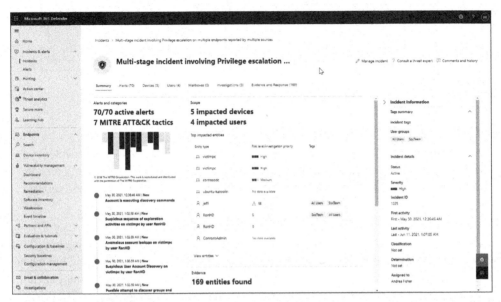

FIGURE 3-16 Incident details

Automated Investigation and Remediation (AIR) is a SOAR technology that uses various inspection algorithms to follow SOC-based processes to examine alerts and take immediate action. When a security alert is triggered, AIR automatically starts investigating the device. Depending on the organization's configuration, AIR can wait for approval to take action, such as deleting a malicious file or automatically taking action. In addition, AIR can recommend or act on one or several actions, such as stopping a service, removing a scheduled task, and so on. AIR reduces the workload on the SOC by automating investigation processes.

Normally, an SOC analyst would need to take these steps and actions on the endpoints, which can be cumbersome. MSDE provides management capabilities to onboard devices, and it is fully integrated with Microsoft Endpoint Manager and Azure Defender for servers, which provides a complete, end-to-end experience for configuration, deployment, and monitoring. MSDE also provides Role-Based Access Control (RBAC), which gives you fine-grained control over which resources users and entities can access. MSDE has a rich set of APIs, allowing you to automate workflows and integrate with other applications in the organization's environment. Figure 3-17 shows an overview of the MSDE APIs.

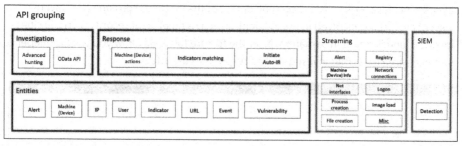

FIGURE 3-17 Defender for Endpoint APIs

Microsoft Defender for Cloud Apps

Microsoft Defender for Cloud Apps is a cloud-access security broker (CASB) that provides multiple capabilities, including XDR for SOC, governance and policy, data protection, and session monitoring. Defender for Cloud Apps provides rich visibility into your cloud apps and services and control over data and analytics to detect threats across your cloud services.

Defender for Cloud Apps allows you to discover and control the use of Shadow IT. By analyzing your cloud traffic logs, you can discover IaaS, PaaS, and SaaS services being used across the organization. Some of these apps might be known and controlled already, but many organizations are unaware of all the cloud services being consumed, which means they cannot control and protect them. MCAS can analyze firewall and proxy logs or integrate with Microsoft Defender for Endpoint to see the traffic to which endpoints are connecting. Let's take a look at the Discovery dashboard by following these steps:

1. Open a browser, navigate to *security.microsoft.com*, and sign in with a user who has **Security Administrator** privileges.

2. Click the **Cloud Discovery** item in the left menu under **Cloud Apps**.

3. Figure 3-18 shows the **Cloud Discovery** dashboard. Here, you can see an overview of all the discovered cloud apps and services. You can see a count of apps, IPs, users, devices, and traffic. Also, you can see a breakdown of cloud apps by category and risk. Also, you can see the discovered apps and entities using those applications.

Once cloud apps are discovered, they can be connected to Defender for Cloud Apps to monitor and apply policies. Defender for Cloud Apps provides connections for the following apps:

- Azure
- Amazon Web Services
- Box
- Dropbox
- GitHub
- Google Workspace

- Google Cloud Platform
- Office 365
- Okta
- Salesforce
- ServiceNow
- WebEx
- Workday

FIGURE 3-18 Cloud Discovery dashboard

Once connected, Defender for Cloud Apps can apply policy control over the cloud app. Defender for Cloud Apps provides the following policy types:

- **Access** Provides real-time monitoring and control over log-ins to your cloud apps
- **Activity** Allows the monitoring and enforcement of activities in your cloud apps
- **Anomaly detection** Looks for unusual activities in your cloud apps
- **App discovery** Alerts you when new apps are detected in the organization
- **Cloud discovery anomaly detection** Looks for unusual activities in cloud discovery logs
- **File** Scans cloud apps for files, file types, or data and applies governance actions
- **Malware** Identifies malicious files in cloud storage
- **OAuth app anomaly detection** Looks for unusual OAuth app activity
- **OAuth App** Creates an alert when risky OAuth apps are detected
- **Session** Provides real-time monitoring and control over user activity in cloud apps

Microsoft Defender for Identity

Microsoft Defender for Identity, sometimes called MSDI, is a cloud-based security solution for monitoring Windows Server Active Directory and Active Directory Federation Services (ADFS). It can identify, detect, and allow the investigation of advanced threats and compromised identities or malicious insiders.

Defender for identity uses a sensor that can be installed on Active Directory Domain Controllers or Active Directory Federation Servers to collect data from event logs, network traffic, and Active Directory. As data is collected, Defender for Identity

- Detects an attack through specific detections
- Collects and analyzes the data to create behavioral baselines for each user
- Builds mappings of activities, permissions, and group memberships

This process allows the security analyst to understand the attack better regarding the identity. The analyst can see both the alert and understand the identity's patterns via a created graph showing the attack's lateral movement paths across the environment. Lateral movement is a typical attack technique that uses credentials to pivot from one part of the network to another.

Microsoft Defender Vulnerability Management

Microsoft Defender Vulnerability Management helps you by delivering asset visibility, intelligent assessment, and built-in remediation for assets across your environment. Vulnerabilities are the largest attack surface available to an attacker. These need to be managed, triaged, and resolved or mitigated. Defender Vulnerability Management provides an easy way for you to achieve this. It provides three core capabilities:

- Continuous discovery
- Risk-based intelligent prioritization
- Remediation and tracking

Defender Vulnerability Management has built-in agentless scanners that continuously scan and detect risks. Consolidated inventories provide a real-time view of your organization's software applications, digital certificates, hardware and firmware, and browser extensions to help you monitor and assess all your organization's assets.

Defender Vulnerability Management leverages Microsoft's threat intelligence, break likelihood, business context, and device assessments to help prioritize vulnerabilities in your organization. A single view is provided with prioritized recommendations to help ensure your organization focuses on what matters most.

Remediation and tracking are provided by sending a remediation task in Microsoft Intune or allowing the blocking of vulnerable applications.

Microsoft Defender Threat Intelligence

Microsoft Defender Threat Intelligence provides the ability to research and learn about threats across the Internet, helping security analysts triage and understand incidents and alerts occurring in the environment.

Defender for TI provides narrative articles by Microsoft that provide insight into threat actors, tooling, attacks, and vulnerabilities. The TI articles can provide actionable content and key indicators of compromise to help security analysts take action. Some vulnerability articles share the details of vulnerabilities, such as CVEs. This allows security analysts to understand the vulnerability and affected components, how to mitigate them, and other key observations.

Microsoft centralizes numerous data sets into a single platform, Defender TI, making it easier for Microsoft's community and customers to conduct infrastructure analysis. Microsoft's primary focus is to provide as much data as possible about Internet infrastructure to support a variety of security use cases. This Internet data is categorized into two distinct groups: traditional and advanced.

Traditional data sets include resolutions, WHOIS, SSL Certificates, subdomains, DNS, reverse DNS, and services. Advanced data sets include trackers, components, host pairs, and cookies. Trackers, components, host pairs, and cookies data sets are collected by observing the Document Object Model (DOM) of crawled web pages.

You can also view reputation scoring for hosts, domains, or IP addresses, helping validate known or unknown entities when investigating to quickly understand if something is suspicious or malicious.

Microsoft 365 Defender portal

The Microsoft 365 Defender portal is located at *security.microsoft.com*. All the Defender services are located in the portal. Here, you can find the incidents and alerts to be triaged and investigated. The **Hunting** tab allows you to build custom detection rules and look for specific threats in your environment.

You can also view your Microsoft Secure Score, which represents the organization's security posture across identities, apps, and devices. A **Learning Hub** also provides Defender guidance and reports.

Thought experiment

In this thought experiment, demonstrate your skills and knowledge of the topics covered in this chapter. You can find answers to this thought experiment in the next section.

Contoso project to improve their security posture and incident management

The new head of IT Security wants to split the team into two areas, one focusing on cloud security posture management and the other handling incidents. Regarding security posture management improvement, Contoso needs to adopt a solution that can provide a mechanism to track progress over time. Contoso also wants to make sure that Microsoft security best practices are natively evaluated across their workloads in Azure.

When it comes to the incident response team, they need to adopt an SIEM/SOAR solution that can perform data correlation and data aggregation. The solution also needs to be flexible to allow custom alerts rules to be created.

Contoso still has some Domain Controllers on-premises and wants to ensure that they are protected from the operating system perspective and potential identity attacks.

With this information in mind, answer the following questions:

1. Which solution should Contoso utilize for cloud security posture management based on the prerequisites?
2. Which cloud security posture management capability will allow Contoso to track progress over time in its cloud security improvement journey?
3. Which solution should Contoso use for an SIEM/SOAR?
4. What solutions should be installed on the on-premisis domain controllers?

Thought experiment answers

This section contains the solution to the thought experiment.

1. Microsoft Defender for Cloud
2. Secure Score
3. Microsoft Sentinel
4. Microsoft Defender for Identity and Microsoft Defender for Endpoint

Chapter summary

- The basic protection provides automatic attack mitigations against DDoS; some capabilities are only provided by the DDoS Standard tier.
- Azure Firewall can also span multiple availability zones for increased availability.

112   CHAPTER 3   Capabilities of Microsoft security solutions

- Web Application Firewall (WAF) provides centralized protection of your web applications from common exploits and vulnerabilities.

- Network segmentation is the practice of separating resources for security or application of governance across workloads.

- Network security group (NSG) in Azure enables you to filter network traffic by creating rules that allow or deny inbound network traffic to or outbound network traffic from different types of resources.

- Azure Bastion is a PaaS service that you can deploy to connect to a virtual machine using your browser and the Azure portal.

- Azure Key Vault allows you to store information that should not be made public, such as secrets, certificates, and keys.

- Adopting a cloud security posture management (CSPM) platform helps organizations identify and remediate risks by leveraging this platform to provide visibility, uninterrupted monitoring, and remediation.

- Microsoft Defender for Cloud gives organizations complete visibility and control over cloud workloads' security in Azure, on-premises, or another cloud provider.

- In addition to CSPM capabilities, Defender for Cloud has threat detection options available as part of the Cloud Workload Protection (CWP) plans.

- Security baselines for Azure focus on cloud-centric control areas, where these controls are consistent with well-known security benchmarks, such as those described by the Center for Internet Security (CIS).

- The SIEM can collect logs from various sources using different methods. An agent can be installed on endpoints to collect and send logs locally. A collector can be deployed for systems where agents cannot be installed.

- Security orchestration, automation, and response (SOAR) enables organizations to automate incident response and coordination detection and remediation actions across disparate systems.

- Microsoft Sentinel is the world's first cloud-native SIEM and SOAR solution. It was built from the ground up in the cloud and allows organizations to scale with their SIEM and SOAR demands.

- Defender for Office 365 (MSDO) provides threat protection for inbound messages, links (URLs), and attachments for collaboration tools, including Microsoft Teams, SharePoint Online, OneDrive for Business, and Exchange Online.

- Microsoft Defender for Endpoint (MSDE) protects endpoints, allowing enterprises to prevent, detect, investigate, and respond to advanced threats.

- Microsoft Defender for Cloud Apps is a cloud-access security broker (CASB) that provides multiple capabilities, including XDR for SOC, governance and policy, data protection, and session monitoring.

- Microsoft Defender for Identity, sometimes called MSDI, is a cloud-based security solution for monitoring Windows Server Active Directory and Active Directory Federation Services (ADFS).

- Microsoft Defender Vulnerability Management helps you by delivering asset visibility, intelligent assessment, and built-in remediation for assets across your environment.

- Microsoft Defender Threat Intelligence provides the ability to research and learn about threats across the Internet.

- The Microsoft 365 Defender portal is located at *security.microsoft.com*. All of the Defender services are located in the portal.

CHAPTER 4

Describe the capabilities of Microsoft compliance solutions

Keeping track of the many compliance-related legal and regulatory standards has become increasingly complex over the past decade. The management of personal information is guided by health-related regulations like the Health Insurance Portability and Accountability Act (HIPAA), rules related to student privacy like the Family Educational Rights and Privacy Act (FERPA), and ISO standards like ISO 27701. Microsoft has many compliance solutions that can assist organizations with protecting themselves and their partners as well.

Skills covered in this chapter:

- Skill 4.1: Service Trust portal and privacy
- Skill 4.2: Common compliance needs
- Skill 4.3: Information protection, data lifecyle management, and data governance
- Skill 4.4: Insider risk, eDiscovery, and auditing

Skill 4.1: Service Trust Portal and privacy

Microsoft Cloud services are built on a foundation of trust, security, and compliance. The Microsoft Service Trust Portal offers a range of content, tools, and resources covering Microsoft's security, privacy, and compliance practices. Microsoft also helps organizations fulfill their privacy requirements through Microsoft Priva. Priva assists organizations in protecting personal data and establishing a workplace resilient to privacy concerns. This section covers the skills necessary to describe the Service Trust Portal and privacy principles according to the Exam SC-900 outline.

Microsoft's Service Trust Portal

The Microsoft Service Trust Portal offers diverse content, tools, and resources explaining how Microsoft cloud services safeguard your data and how you can oversee cloud data security and compliance for your organization. The Service Trust Portal (STP) serves as Microsoft's public platform for sharing audit reports and other compliance-related materials linked to

Microsoft's cloud services. Users of STP can access audit reports generated by external auditors and glean insights from whitepapers authored by Microsoft. These resources delve into how Microsoft cloud services protect your data and guide your organization's cloud data security and compliance.

> **This skill covers how to:**
> - Access and utilize Microsoft's Service Trust Portal
> - Understand Microsoft's privacy principles
> - Utilize Microsoft Priva, including Priva privacy risk management and subject rights requests

Accessing the Service Trust Portal

To utilize certain resources on the Service Trust Portal, you need to log in as an authenticated user with your Microsoft cloud services account (Microsoft Entra organization account). Additionally, you are required to review and agree to the Microsoft nondisclosure agreement for Compliance Materials.

On the Service Trust Portal landing page, you'll find content neatly categorized into the following sections:

- **Certifications, Regulations, and Standards** In the STP certifications, regulations, and standards section, you will find information about security implementation and design. The primary goal is to facilitate your efforts to meet regulatory compliance objectives by offering insights into how Microsoft Cloud services ensure the security of your data.

- **Reports, Whitepapers, and Artifacts** This section contains general documents covering a range of categories, including
  - Documents focusing on business continuity and disaster recovery (BCP and DR), providing valuable insights into strategies and practices to ensure operational resilience.
  - Information detailing the attestation of penetration tests and security assessments carried out by third-party entities.
  - Resources specifically addressing privacy and data protection, offering guidelines and materials to assist in navigating and adhering to privacy regulations.
  - A compilation of whitepapers and comprehensive answers to frequently asked questions, serving as a valuable knowledge base for users seeking in-depth information on various topics.

- **Industry and Regional Resources** This section is comprised of documents tailored to specific industries and regions, providing targeted information for diverse contexts, including

- Resources that delve into regulatory compliance guidance for the Financial Services Industry (FSI) are categorized by country or region to address the unique requirements of each locality.

- Documentation outlining the capabilities offered by Microsoft to cater to the unique needs and compliance standards of the Healthcare and Life Sciences industry.

- Industry-specific resources focusing on the Media and Entertainment sector, offering insights and guidance related to compliance and security in this domain.

- Exclusive resources designed specifically for United States government customers, providing information tailored to US government entities' regulatory landscape and compliance requirements.

- Documents related to the compliance of Microsoft's online services with various regional policies and regulations.

- **Resources for your Organization**   This section compiles documents pertinent to your organization, with restricted access based on your organization's subscription and permissions.

My Library

The **My Library** feature of the **Service Trust Portal** allows you to add relevant documents and resources to a personalized My Library page. This convenient functionality allows you to access all pertinent documents in one central location. To add a document to your **My Library**, simply navigate to the ellipsis (**...**) menu next to a document and choose **Save To Library**.

Additionally, the notifications feature allows you to stay informed about updates to documents in your **My Library**. You can configure **My Library** to send email notifications when Microsoft updates a document you've saved. **Notification Settings** in **My Library** allows you to customize the frequency of notifications and specify an email address within your organization to receive these updates. These email notifications include links to the updated documents and briefly describe the changes.

When a document is part of a series, you will be subscribed to the series and receive notifications whenever there's an update, ensuring that you are informed and have easy access to the latest information relevant to your organization's needs.

EXAM TIP

Make sure you understand the various sections of the **Service Trust Portal**, the types of documents you can find in each section, and how to save documents and get update notifications.

Microsoft's privacy principles

Microsoft's products and services run on trust. Microsoft is strongly committed to valuing, protecting, and defending privacy, operating under principles prioritizing user control, transparency, security, legal protections, non-content-based targeting, and delivering tangible benefits to users.

As defined in the Microsoft Privacy Statement, Microsoft's approach to privacy is built on the following six principles:

- **Control** Microsoft's philosophy revolves around controlling the customer's data and privacy. Microsoft provides user-friendly tools and clear choices, ensuring that individuals have access to, can modify, or can delete their data at any time. Microsoft commits to not using data without an explicit agreement, utilizing it solely to deliver the services the user chooses. Compliance with privacy laws and standards reinforces users' control over their data.

- **Transparency** Microsoft is dedicated to being transparent about data collection and use, enabling users to make informed decisions. Data processing only occurs with user agreement and adherence to stringent policies and procedures. Subcontractors or subprocessors engaged by Microsoft adhere to contractual privacy commitments, ensuring that they can only perform functions assigned by Microsoft. The Service Trust Portal provides detailed resources, including the Microsoft Online Services Subprocessor List, which identifies authorized subprocessors who have been audited against stringent security and privacy requirements in advance.

- **Security** The safeguarding of entrusted data is a top priority for Microsoft. Utilizing state-of-the-art encryption, the company protects data both at rest and in transit. Multiple encryption layers fortify against unauthorized access, and Microsoft employs technologies like Azure Key Vault to help you control access to passwords, encryption keys, and other secrets.

- **Strong legal protections** Microsoft is committed to respecting local privacy laws and considers privacy a fundamental human right. Microsoft defends data through well-defined response policies, contractual commitments, and, if necessary, legal action. Government requests for data are directed to the user, and Microsoft scrutinizes such demands to ensure legality and appropriateness. Users are promptly notified of any data requests unless legally prohibited, and Microsoft challenges government requests for data where we can lawfully do so.

- **No content-based targeting** Microsoft categorically avoids using personal content, such as email, chat, or files, for targeted advertising. User data is not shared with advertiser-supported services, and mining for purposes like marketing research or advertising is strictly prohibited.

- **Benefits to you** When Microsoft collects data, it is to benefit the user. Microsoft includes troubleshooting to prevent, detect, and repair service-related problems, improving features to enhance reliability and protection, and providing personalized enhancements for a better overall customer experience.

These principles form the foundation of Microsoft's privacy commitment, influencing the design and operation of its products and services.

EXAM TIP

Know the six principles that Microsoft's approach to privacy is built upon.

Microsoft Priva

In today's data landscape, privacy has become a foremost concern for both organizations and consumers. Increasing regulations and laws worldwide underscored the growing apprehension about handling private data. These regulations set clear guidelines for organizations regarding the storage of personal data and grant individuals the right to manage the personal data that organizations collect.

Organizations must adopt a "privacy by default" approach to align with regulatory requirements and instill customer trust. Instead of relying on manual processes and a fragmented set of tools, a comprehensive solution is essential to address common challenges, including

- **Employee Training** Assisting employees in adopting sound data-handling practices and providing training to identify and rectify potential issues.
- **Risk Assessment** Understanding the potential risks associated with the quantity and nature of personal data stored and shared by the organization.
- **Data Subject Requests** Efficiently and timely fulfillment of data subject requests or subject rights requests, ensuring compliance with regulations.

Microsoft Priva is a solution to tackle these challenges, enabling organizations to achieve their privacy objectives. Priva offers capabilities through two distinct solutions:

- **Priva Privacy Risk Management** Provides visibility into an organization's data and offers policy templates designed to mitigate risks
- **Priva Subject Rights Requests** Focuses on automation and workflow tools, streamlining the process of fulfilling data requests

Priva privacy risk management

Microsoft Priva plays a crucial role in enhancing your organization's understanding of stored data by automating the discovery of personal data assets and offering insightful visualizations of key information. These visualizations are conveniently accessible on the overview and data profile pages, which are currently accessible through the Microsoft Purview compliance portal. Through this integration, Priva facilitates a comprehensive and visual representation of your organization's data landscape, empowering you to make informed decisions easily and manage personal data assets effectively.

The overview dashboard serves as a comprehensive window into your organization's data within Microsoft 365. Designed for privacy administrators, this dashboard offers a holistic perspective, allowing for monitoring trends and activities. It equips administrators to identify and investigate potential risks associated with personal data. The overview dashboard also serves as a launching pad for essential activities such as policy management and actions related to subject rights requests.

The data profile page offers a snapshot view, concisely overviewing your organization's personal data within Microsoft 365 and its specific locations. This page is a valuable resource, offering insight into the types of data your organization houses. By offering a comprehensive snapshot, the data profile page becomes an essential tool for organizations to understand the nature and distribution of personal data within the Microsoft 365 ecosystem.

Priva assesses the data within your Microsoft 365 tenant, evaluating information stored across various Microsoft 365 services. These services include

- Exchange Online
- SharePoint Online
- OneDrive for Business
- Microsoft Teams

Privacy Risk Management in Microsoft Priva empowers you to establish policies to identify and address privacy risks within your Microsoft 365 environment. These policies serve as internal guidelines, aiding you in

- **Detecting overexposed personal data** Identify instances where personal data is overexposed, enabling users to take necessary measures to secure and restrict access to it.

- **Limiting transfers of personal data** Spot and control the transfers of personal data across different departments or regional borders, ensuring compliance with privacy regulations and internal policies.

- **Reducing unused personal data** Assist users in identifying and minimizing the amount of unused personal data stored within your environment. This proactive approach helps optimize data storage and adhere to privacy best practices.

By utilizing Privacy Risk Management policies in Microsoft Priva, your organization can proactively manage and mitigate potential privacy risks, fostering a secure and compliant data environment within the Microsoft 365 ecosystem.

Priva Subject Rights Requests

Many global privacy regulations grant individuals (or data subjects) the right to make review requests or manage the personal data that companies have collected about them. These requests are known by various terms, including data subject requests (DSRs), data subject access requests (DSARs), or consumer rights requests. However, locating relevant data for these requests can be complex for companies dealing with vast amounts of information.

Microsoft Priva offers a robust solution to address these inquiries through its Subject Rights Requests solution. This feature provides essential workflow, automation, and collaboration capabilities to assist organizations in efficiently managing these requests. It streamlines the process of searching for subject data, reviewing findings, collecting pertinent files, and generating comprehensive reports. By leveraging the Subject Rights Requests solution in Microsoft Priva, organizations can navigate the complexities of data subject requests, ensuring a streamlined and compliant approach to handling these privacy inquiries.

Skill 4.2: Common compliance needs

While managing compliance is a difficult subject covered by numerous regulations and standards, Microsoft has built-in tools and capabilities to help address this complexity. In this section, we will discover some of these tools and discuss how they can help customers protect their sensitive information, manage data governance, and respond to regulatory requests promptly. This section covers the skills necessary to describe common compliance needs according to the Exam SC-900 outline.

> **This skill covers how to:**
> - Access and navigate the features of the Microsoft Purview compliance portal
> - Understand the use of the Microsoft Purview Compliance Manager
> - Understand Compliance Score

Microsoft Purview compliance portal

The Microsoft Purview compliance portal provides quick access to the data and tools your organization needs to manage compliance. One of the most difficult challenges regarding compliance is finding all the information you need in a central location. The compliance portal is a nexus that combines all the various compliance tools Microsoft provides and can help you understand where to go next.

When you log into the compliance portal, it presents you with introductory information and cards related to compliance management across Microsoft Purview, as shown in Figure 4-1.

FIGURE 4-1 Microsoft Purview compliance portal home page

These cards visually represent your organization's current data compliance posture, various solutions available to your organization, and a summary of active alerts related to compliance. In addition to the cards presented in the compliance portal, the navigation pane on the left side provides access to additional information and solutions to help manage compliance. The following areas are available via the navigation pane:

- **Home**   Returns you to the Microsoft Purview compliance portal main page.
- **Compliance Manager**   Allows you to check your **Compliance Score** and manage compliance for your organization.
- **Data Classification**   Provides access to trainable classifiers, sensitive information type entity definitions, the Content Explorer, and Activity Explorer.
- **Data Connectors**   Allows you to configure connectors to import and archive data in your Microsoft 365 subscription.
- **Alerts**   Provides access to view and resolve active alerts.
- **Policies**   Allows you to establish policies to govern data and manage devices and provides access to both DLP and retention policies.
- **Roles & Scopes**   Provides options for managing who can access the Microsoft Purview compliance portal to view content or complete tasks. Additional information related to role and scope management will be provided later in this section.
- **Trials**   Provides information on security and compliance capabilities in Microsoft 365 Defender and Microsoft Purview, which can be tested for free.
- **Catalog**   Provides information about the compliance and risk management solutions available to your organization.
- **Audit**   Shows the Audit Log, allowing users to investigate common support and compliance issues.
- **Content Search**   Allows you to find email in Exchange mailboxes, documents in SharePoint sites and OneDrive locations, and instant messaging conversations in Microsoft Teams and Skype for Business.
- **Communication Compliance**   Provides options for minimizing communication risks by automating the capture of inappropriate messages, investigating possible policy violations, and taking remedial steps.
- **Data Loss Prevention**   Allows you to create rules to detect sensitive content being used and shared throughout your organization, both in the cloud and on devices, and helps to prevent accidental data loss.
- **eDiscovery**   Provides both core and eDiscovery (Premium) options for preserving, collecting, reviewing, analyzing, and exporting content related to your organization's internal and external investigations.
- **Information Governance**   Allows you to manage your content lifecycle with features to import, store, and classify business-critical data.

- **Information Protection** Provides configuration of sensitivity labels and policies to discover, classify, and protect sensitive and business-critical content throughout its lifecycle.

- **Insider Risk Management** Allows you to detect risky activity across your organization to help you quickly identify, investigate, and act on insider risks and threats.

- **Records Management** Allows you to configure the retention schedule for regulatory, legal, and business-critical records in your organization.

- **Privacy Risk Management** A function of Microsoft Priva that allows you to set up policies that identify privacy risks in your Microsoft 365 environment and enable easy remediation.

- **Subject Rights Requests** A function of Microsoft Priva that allows you to respond to subject rights requests by finding and exporting users' personal data using automation, insights, and workflows.

As you can see, the compliance portal provides quick access to many different areas related to compliance in Microsoft 365. We will discuss several of these areas in further detail throughout this chapter.

Permissions in the Microsoft Purview compliance portal

The Microsoft Purview compliance portal supports directly managing permissions for users who perform compliance tasks in Microsoft 365. From the roles & scopes tab in the navigation pane, you can manage both Entra ID and Microsoft Purview dedicated roles, as shown in Figure 4-2.

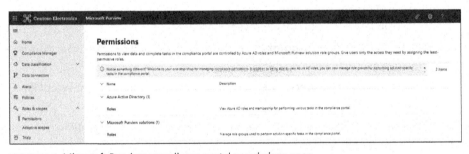

FIGURE 4-2 Microsoft Purview compliance portal permissions page

To view the **Permissions** tab in the Microsoft Purview compliance portal, users need to be a global administrator or be assigned the **Role Management** role. The available Entra ID roles were described earlier in this book in Skill 2.3. This section will focus on the Microsoft Purview role groups. Role groups are role-based access control (RBAC) permission groups with the appropriate roles for accessing the various functions within the Microsoft Purview compliance portal. The following role groups exist in the compliance portal:

- **Attack Simulator Administrators** Don't use this role group in these portals. Use the corresponding role in Microsoft Entra ID.

- **Attack Simulator Payload Authors** Don't use this role group in these portals. Use the corresponding role in Microsoft Entra ID.
- **Audit Manager** Manage audit log settings and search, view, and export Audit Logs.
- **Audit Reader** Search, view, and export audit logs.
- **Billing Administrator** Configure billing features.
- **Communication Compliance** Provides permission to all the communication compliance roles: **Administrator**, **Analyst**, **Investigator**, and **Viewer**.
- **Communication Compliance Administrators** Administrators of communication compliance who can create/edit policies and define global settings.
- **Communication Compliance Analysts** Analysts of communication compliance that can investigate policy matches, view message metadata, and take remediation actions.
- **Communication Compliance Investigators** Analysts of communication compliance who can investigate policy matches, view message content, and take remediation actions.
- **Communication Compliance Viewers** Viewer of communication compliance that can access the available reports and widgets.
- **Compliance Administrator** Members can manage settings for device management, data loss prevention, reports, and preservation.
- **Compliance Data Administrator** Members can manage settings for device management, data protection, data loss prevention, reports, and preservation.
- **Compliance Manager Administrators** Manage template creation and modification.
- **Compliance Manager Assessors** Create assessments, implement improvement actions, and update test status for improvement actions.
- **Compliance Manager Contributors** Create assessments and perform work to implement improvement actions.
- **Compliance Manager Readers** View all **Compliance Manager** content except for administrator functions.
- **Content Explorer Content Viewer** View the content files in Content Explorer.
- **Content Explorer List Viewer** View all items in Content Explorer in list format only.
- **Data Catalog Curators** Perform create, read, modify, and delete actions on catalog data objects and establish relationships between objects.
- **Data Estate Insights Admins** Provides admin access to all insights reports across platforms and providers.
- **Data Estate Insights Readers** Provides read-only access to all insights reports across platforms and providers.
- **Data Investigator** Perform searches on mailboxes, SharePoint Online sites, and OneDrive for Business locations.
- **Data Source Administrators** Manage data sources and data scans.

- **eDiscovery Manager** Members can perform searches and place holds on Exchange mailboxes, SharePoint Online sites, and OneDrive for Business locations. Members can also create and manage eDiscovery cases, add and remove members to a case, create and edit Content Searches associated with a case, and access case data in eDiscovery (Premium). An eDiscovery Administrator is a member of the eDiscovery Manager role group who has been assigned additional permissions. The primary difference between an eDiscovery Manager and an eDiscovery Administrator is that an eDiscovery Administrator can access all cases listed on the compliance portal's eDiscovery Cases page. An eDiscovery manager can only access the cases they created or cases they're a member of. In addition to the tasks that an eDiscovery Manager can perform, an eDiscovery Administrator can

    - View all eDiscovery cases in the organization.

    - Manage any eDiscovery case after they add themselves as a case member.

- **Exact Data Match Upload Admins** Upload data for Exact Data Match.

- **Global Reader** Members have read-only access to reports and alerts and can see all the configurations and settings. The primary difference between Global Reader and Security Reader is that a Global Reader can access configuration and settings.

- **Information Protection** Full control over all information protection features, including sensitivity labels and their policies, DLP, all classifier types, Activity Explorer, Content Explorers, and all related reports.

- **Information Protection Admins** Create, edit, and delete DLP policies, sensitivity labels and their policies, and all classifier types. Manage endpoint DLP settings and simulation mode for auto-labeling policies.

- **Information Protection Analysts** Access and manage DLP alerts and Activity Explorer. View-only access to DLP policies, sensitivity labels and their policies, and all classifier types.

- **Information Protection Investigators** Access and manage DLP alerts, Activity Explorer, and Content Explorer. View-only access to DLP policies, sensitivity labels and their policies, and all classifier types.

- **Information Protection Readers** View-only access to reports for DLP policies and sensitivity labels and their policies.

- **Insider Risk Management** Use this role group to manage Insider Risk Management for your organization in a single group. You can configure Insider Risk Management permissions in a single group by adding all user accounts for designated administrators, analysts, and investigators. This role group contains all Insider Risk Management permission roles. This role group is the easiest way to get started with Insider Risk Management quickly and is a good fit for organizations that don't need separate permissions defined for separate groups of users.

- **Insider Risk Management Admins**   Use this role group to initially configure Insider Risk Management and later to segregate insider risk administrators into a defined group. Users in this role group can create, read, update, and delete Insider Risk Management policies, global settings, and role group assignments.

- **Insider Risk Management Analysts**   Use this group to assign permissions to users who will act as insider risk case analysts. Users in this role group can access all Insider Risk Management alerts, cases, and notices templates. They cannot access the Insider Risk Content Explorer.

- **Insider Risk Management Approvers**   For internal approval use only.

- **Insider Risk Management Auditors**   Use this group to assign permissions to users that will audit Insider Risk Management activities. Users in this role group can access the insider risk Audit Log.

- **Insider Risk Management Investigators**   Use this group to assign permissions to users who will act as insider risk data investigators. Users in this role group can access all Insider Risk Management alerts, cases, notices templates, and the Content Explorer for all cases.

- **Insider Risk Management Session Approvers**   For internal approval use only.

- **IRM Contributors**   This role group is visible but is used by background services only.

- **Knowledge Administrators**   Configure knowledge and learning, assign training, and other intelligent features.

- **MailFlow Administrator**   Members can monitor and view mail flow insights and reports in the Defender portal. Global Administrators can add ordinary users to this group, but if the user isn't a member of the Exchange Administrators group, the user doesn't have access to Exchange Administrator–related tasks.

- **Organization Management**   Members can control permissions for accessing features in these portals and manage settings for device management, data loss prevention, reports, and preservation. Users who aren't Global Administrators must be Exchange Administrators to see and take action on devices managed by Basic Mobility and Security for Microsoft 365 (formerly known as Mobile Device Management or MDM). Global Administrators are automatically added as members of this role group, but you don't see them in the output of the Get-RoleGroupMember cmdlet in Security & Compliance PowerShell.

- **Privacy Management**   Manage access control for Privacy Management solutions in the Microsoft Purview compliance portal.

- **Privacy Management Administrators**   Administrators of privacy management solutions that can create/edit policies and define global settings.

- **Privacy Management Analysts**   Analysts of privacy management solutions that can investigate policy matches, view message metadata, and take remediation actions.

- **Privacy Management Contributors**   Manage contributor access for privacy management cases.

- **Privacy Management Investigators**   Investigators of privacy management solutions that can investigate policy matches, view message content, and take remediation actions.

- **Privacy Management Viewers**   Viewer of privacy management solution that can access the available dashboards and widgets.

- **Purview Administrators**   Create, edit, and delete domains and perform role assignments.

- **Quarantine Administrator**   Members can access all quarantine actions.

- **Records Management**   Members can configure all records management aspects, including retention labels and disposition reviews.

- **Reviewer**   Members can access review sets in eDiscovery (Premium) cases. Members of this role group can see and open the list of cases on the **eDiscovery** > **Advanced** page in the Microsoft Purview compliance portal that they're members of. After the user accesses an eDiscovery (Premium) case, they can select Review sets to access case data. This role doesn't allow the user to preview the results of a collection search associated with the case or do other search or case management tasks. Members of this role group can only access the data in a review set.

- **Security Administrator**   Members can access many security features of Identity Protection Center, Privileged Identity Management, Monitor Microsoft 365 Service Health, the Defender portal, and the Purview compliance portal. By default, this role group may not appear to have any members. However, the Security Administrator role from Microsoft Entra ID is assigned to this role group. Therefore, this role group inherits the capabilities and membership of the Security Administrator role from Microsoft Entra ID. To manage permissions centrally, add and remove group members in the Microsoft Entra admin center. If you edit this role group in these portals (membership or roles), those changes apply only to the security and compliance areas and not to any other services. This role group includes all of the read-only permissions of the Security reader role and additional administrative permissions for the same services: Azure Information Protection, Identity Protection Center, Privileged Identity Management, Monitor Microsoft 365 Service Health, the Defender portal, and the Purview compliance portal.

- **Security Operator**   Members can manage security alerts and view reports and settings of security features.

- **Security Reader**   Members have read-only access to many security features of Identity Protection Center, Privileged Identity Management, Monitor Microsoft 365 Service Health, and the Defender and compliance portals. By default, this role group may not appear to have any members. However, the Security Reader role from Microsoft Entra ID is assigned to this role group. Therefore, this role group inherits the capabilities and membership of the Security Reader role from Microsoft Entra ID. To manage permissions centrally, add and remove group members in the Microsoft Entra admin center. If you edit this role group in the portals (membership or roles), those changes apply only to security and compliance areas and not to any other services.

- **Service Assurance User**   Members can access the Service assurance section in the compliance portal. Service assurance provides reports and documents describing Microsoft's security practices for customer data stored in Microsoft 365. It also provides independent third-party audit reports on Microsoft 365.
- **Subject Rights Request Administrators**   Create subject rights requests.
- **Subject Rights Request Approvers**   Approvers who can approve subject rights requests.
- **Supervisory Review**   Members can create and manage the policies that define which communications are subject to review in an organization.

> **MORE INFO   ROLE GROUPS**
>
> To see additional information regarding the roles included in each of the role groups, visit *https://aka.ms/SC900_ComplianceRoleGroups.*

EXAM TIP

Different role groups allow access to specific areas of the Microsoft Purview compliance portal. Understand which role groups are required for access to these areas.

Microsoft Purview Compliance Manager

Microsoft Purview Compliance Manager can be accessed via the navigation menu in the Microsoft Purview compliance portal. This feature allows you to manage your organization's compliance requirements by providing an inventory of your data protection risks, supplying pre built and custom assessments to help your organization comply with common industry and regional standards and regulations, and guiding you to improvement actions that can help increase your **Compliance Score**. **Compliance Manager** provides step-by-step guidance to assist organizations with implementing regulatory requirements and helps to translate compli-cated regulations into simple language.

Compliance Manager is broken down into four key elements: **Controls**, **Assessments**, **Regulations**, and **Improvement Actions**. When navigating to **Compliance Manager**, you start on the **Overview** page, as shown in Figure 4-3.

The **Overview** page shows the **Compliance Manager** dashboard, which displays your organization's current **Compliance Score**, draws your attention to areas of improvement, and lists **Key Improvement Actions**. When first accessing the **Compliance Manager**, your **Com-pliance Score** is based on the Microsoft 365 data protection baseline. This baseline is a set of controls that includes common industry regulations and standards.

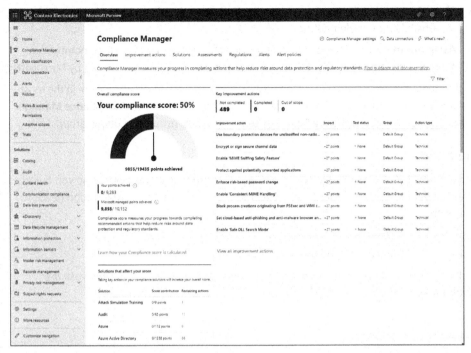

FIGURE 4-3 Compliance Manager Overview page

Controls

A control is a requirement of a regulation, standard, or policy. These controls define how you can assess and manage system configuration, the organizational process, and responsible parties for meeting specific requirements. **Compliance Manager** tracks three kinds of controls: Microsoft-managed controls, your controls, and shared controls.

Microsoft-managed controls are controls related to Microsoft cloud services. Microsoft is responsible for the implementation of these controls. Your controls—also called customer-managed controls—are implemented and managed by your organization. Finally, shared controls are those that both your organization and Microsoft share the responsibility for implementing.

Assessments

Assessments are groupings of controls related to a specific regulation, standard, or policy. Assessments are comprised of five components:

- **In-scope services**   The specific set of Microsoft services applicable to the assessment
- **Microsoft managed controls**   Controls for Microsoft cloud services, which Microsoft implements on your behalf
- **Your controls**   Sometimes referred to as customer-managed controls, these are controls implemented and managed by your organization

- **Shared controls** These are controls that both your organization and Microsoft share responsibility for implementing
- **Assessment score** Shows your progress in achieving the total possible points from actions within the assessment that are managed by your organization and by Microsoft

Assessments may be assigned to custom groups that allow you to organize them in the most logical way for your organization. These groups can then filter results in the **Compliance Manager** dashboard to see your **Compliance Score** related to a specific group or multiple groups.

Regulations

Over 360 regulatory templates are provided within **Compliance Manager** to help you quickly and easily create assessments for specific regulations or standards your organization needs to comply with.

> **MORE INFO   COMPLIANCE MANAGER REGULATIONS**
>
> A full list of the available Compliance Manager regulations can be found at *https://aka.ms/SC900_CMRegulations*.

Improvement actions

Improvement actions provide recommended guidance intended to help you align with data protection regulations and standards. These actions can be assigned to your organization's users for testing and implementation. Improvement actions can also be used to store evidence, status updates, documentation, and notes related to the activity.

The **Improvement Actions** page contains a list of actions your organization can take to improve its **Compliance Score**. These actions can be filtered to show actions related to specific regulations, solutions, groups, categories, the current test status, and to whom the improvement action has been assigned. Figure 4-4 shows some improvement actions that you may see on the **Improvement Actions** tab in **Compliance Manager**.

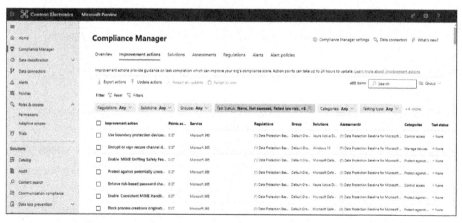

FIGURE 4-4 Compliance Manager Improvement Actions page

EXAM TIP

Make sure you know the key elements of **Compliance Manager** and how they are used.

Compliance Score

Compliance Score was mentioned several times in the previous section because it is part of the **Compliance Manager**, and several tools in **Compliance Manager** can help to improve **Compliance Score**. For the exam, you need to understand the purpose of **Compliance Score** and its benefits to your organization.

The overall **Compliance Score** for your organization is displayed in the **Compliance Manager dashboard**, as shown earlier in Figure 4-3. This score is initially based on the Microsoft 365 data protection baseline, which is a set of controls that includes key regulations and standards for data protection and general data governance. In addition to the overall score displayed in the **Compliance Manager dashboard**, there is a detailed **Compliance Score Breakdown** that shows your organization's **Compliance Score** for each compliance category. An example of this is shown in Figure 4-5.

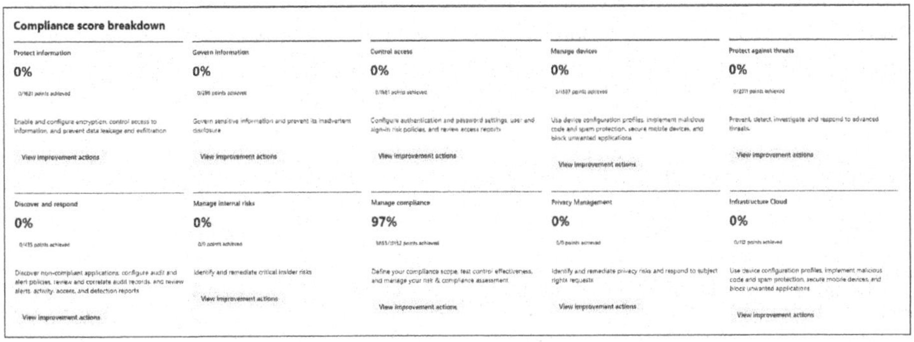

FIGURE 4-5 Compliance Score Breakdown

Understanding Compliance Score

Compliance Score is calculated using points assigned to actions that your organization or Microsoft can take to improve your compliance posture. Actions are grouped based on whether they are technical or non technical, and their impact on **Compliance Score** differs by type. Technical actions are completed by interacting with the technology of a solution. An example could be changing a configuration; this type of action only grants points once, regardless of the number of groups the action belongs to. Non technical actions are implemented without interacting with the technology of a solution and are categorized as documentation or operational actions. These actions are applied at the group level; thus, you will receive points each time this action is taken, even if the action exists in multiple groups.

The scores assigned to various actions are based on whether they are mandatory or discretionary and if they are preventative, detective, or corrective actions. Actions that are mandatory and preventative have the highest score value.

- **Mandatory actions** Can't be bypassed intentionally or accidentally. An example of a mandatory action is a centrally managed password policy that sets requirements for password length, complexity, and expiration. Users must follow these requirements to access the system.

- **Discretionary actions** Relies on users to understand and adhere to a policy; for example, requiring users to lock their computers when unattended is discretionary because it relies on the user.

- **Preventative actions** Address specific risks. For example, protecting information at rest using encryption is a preventative action against attacks and breaches. Separation of duties is a preventative action to manage conflict of interest and guard against fraud.

- **Detective actions** Actively monitor systems to identify irregularities that could represent risks or be used to detect breaches or intrusions. Examples of these types of actions are system access or regulatory compliance audits.

- **Corrective actions** Help admins to minimize the adverse effects of security incidents by undertaking corrective measures to reduce their immediate effect or possibly even reverse the damage.

Point values for the improvement actions are shown in Table 4-1.

TABLE 4-1 Improvement actions point values

	Mandatory	Discretionary
Preventative	+27	+9
Detective	+3	+1
Corrective	+3	+1

Compliance Score is weighted in this manner to help guide organizations to actions that will have a high impact on their compliance posture.

EXAM TIP

Make sure you understand how **Compliance Score** is calculated and the number of points you can receive based on technical versus non technical actions (points count only once for technical actions but can count multiple times for different groups for non technical actions) and point values for preventative actions.

Skill 4.3: Information protection, data lifecycle management, and data governance

Today's organizations are faced with the proliferation of data on a scale never seen. There are many regulations around information handling today, and more are coming out each year. Organizations are faced with the daunting task of controlling their data estate and organizing decades' worth of existing data while also handling new data created daily. Microsoft provides many tools and solutions to protect and govern this information. This section of the chapter covers the skills necessary to describe the various capabilities of Microsoft Information Protection, Data Lifecycle Management, and Data and Governance according to the Exam SC-900 outline.

This skill covers how to:

- Understand Microsoft's data classification capabilities and the types of classifiers that are available

- Access and use Content Explorer and Activity Explorer

- Use sensitivity labels to label and protect sensitive structured and unstructured data

- Use data loss prevention policies to safeguard sensitive company data

- Understand endpoint data loss prevention and the available actions that can be taken to secure endpoint data

- Use records management to manage regulatory, legal, and business-critical records

- Utilize retention policies and labels to comply with regulations and reduce risk when facing litigation and security breaches

- Get started with using Microsoft Purview unified data governance to catalog and understand on-premises, multicloud, and SaaS data across the data estate

---

Data classification capabilities

Industry research tells us that we are looking at a never-before-seen volume, velocity, and variety of data and that organizations need to know their data to ensure that it is handled under compliance regulations and standards. Microsoft has several data classification capabilities such as sensitive information types, trainable classifiers, Content Explorer, and Activity Explorer that can help organizations to know their data.

Figure 4-6 shows the **Data Classification** page of the Microsoft Purview compliance portal. The **Overview** tab shows you graphics for the most used sensitive information types found in your data, how sensitivity and retention labels are applied to content, a summary of the most common actions taken on labeled items, and sensitivity- and retention-labeled data by location.

FIGURE 4-6 Data Classification | Overview page in the Microsoft Purview compliance portal

Sensitive information types can be used to identify sensitive information based on specific keywords, functions, or regular expressions. Microsoft Purview has many built-in sensitive information types to help organizations quickly identify sensitive data. Examples include credit card numbers, tax ID numbers, bank account numbers, and health-related information. You can also create custom sensitive information types to identify and classify data specific to your organization, such as employee ID numbers, customer account numbers, or part numbers.

Categorizing and labeling content so it can be protected and handled properly is the starting place for the information protection discipline. Sensitivity and retention labels can be automatically applied to make the content available for use in Microsoft Purview Data Loss Prevention and auto-apply policies for retention labels.

Microsoft Purview has three ways to classify content:

- **Manually** Manual categorization requires human judgment and action. Users and admins categorize content as they encounter it. You can use the pre-existing labels and sensitive information types or custom-created ones. You can then protect the content and manage its disposition.

- **Automated pattern-matching** These categorization mechanisms include finding content by
  - Keywords or metadata values (keyword query language).
  - Using previously identified patterns of sensitive information like Social Security, credit card, or bank account numbers (sensitive information type entity definitions).
  - Recognizing an item because it's a variation on a template (document finger printing).
  - Using the presence of exact strings exact data match.

- **Classifiers** This categorization method is well suited to content that manual or auto-mated pattern-matching methods don't identify easily. This categorization method is more about using a classifier to identify an item based on what the item is, not by elements in the item (pattern matching). A classifier learns how to identify a type of content by looking at hundreds of examples of the content you're interested in identifying.

Classifiers are available to use as a condition for

- Office auto-labeling with sensitivity labels
- Auto-apply retention label policy based on a condition
- Communication compliance
- Sensitivity labels
- Data loss prevention

Types of classifiers

Classifiers may be pre trained or custom trainable, as shown here:

- **Pre trained classifiers**   Microsoft has created and pre trained more than 60 classifiers that you can start using without training them. These classifiers will appear with the **Ready To Use** status.

- **Custom trainable classifiers**   These classifiers are created by your organization and are typically used when classifying data unique to your organization, like specific contracts or legal documents, financial information, or customer records. Creating a custom trainable classifier requires you to provide 50–500 data samples that match the category positively. After the samples have been processed, a prediction model will be created, and you can then test the classifier by giving it both positive and negative samples of the data to ensure it accurately matches the content. You can then provide feedback on the results, verifying whether each prediction is correct, incorrect, or that you are unsure. The classifier will use this feedback to improve the prediction model.

MORE INFO   **PRE-TRAINED CLASSIFIERS**

A complete list of all pre trained classifiers can be found at *https://aka.ms/ SC900_ClassifierDefinitions.*

MORE INFO   **CREATING CUSTOM TRAINABLE CLASSIFIERS**

More details about creating custom trainable classifiers can be found at *https://aka.ms/ SC900_TrainableClassifiers.*

EXAM TIP

Be familiar with the different sensitive information types and pre trained classifiers available for data classification.

Content Explorer and Activity Explorer

Classifying large amounts of data can be daunting, and understanding all that data can be even more difficult. Microsoft has created Content Explorer and Activity Explorer to assist organizations with visualizing large amounts of data, understanding the actions taking place on that data, and even directly accessing the content found.

The Content Explorer shows a consolidated view of data with a sensitivity or retention label assigned or classified as a sensitive information type for your organization. To access Content Explorer, a user must be a member of either the **Content Explorer List Viewer** or **Content Explorer Content Viewer** roles. Content Explorer lets you quickly identify where sensitive data is located across multiple locations, as shown in Figure 4-7.

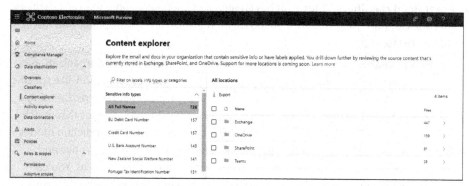

FIGURE 4-7 Content explorer in the Microsoft compliance portal

You can further drill down to specific locations to find documents containing sensitive information and, with appropriate permissions, directly view the matched content in a contextual summary, as shown in Figure 4-8.

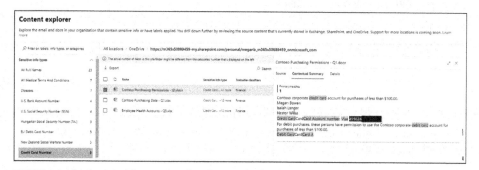

FIGURE 4-8 Viewing specific content using Content Explorer

Activity Explorer supplements the functionality of Content Explorer by showing what activities have occurred on labeled content over time. This can include when documents are read and the users that have accessed those documents, and when labels on documents are changed or downgraded (for instance, going from **Highly Confidential** to **Public**). More than

30 filters are available to help you identify the activities you are interested in, including date range, type of activity, user, DLP policy, and sensitivity or retention labels.

Activity Explorer uses the Microsoft 365 Audit Logs to gather labeling activity information. Label activities tracked include sensitivity and retention label activity from native Office applications, the Azure Information Protection (AIP) unified labeling client and scanner, Exchange Online (sensitivity only), SharePoint Online, and OneDrive. Some tracked label activities include when labels are applied or changed, in auto labeling simulations, when protection is applied or changed, and when files are discovered or read.

> **MORE INFO** **ACTIVITY EXPLORER TRACKED ACTIVITIES**
>
> A full list of label activities tracked by Activity Explorer can be found at *https://aka.ms/ SC900_LabelActivities*.

In addition to labeling activities, Activity Explorer also tracks DLP policy matches from multiple services and locations, including

- Exchange
- SharePoint
- OneDrive
- Teams chat and channels
- On-premises SharePoint folders and libraries
- On-premises file shares
- Windows 10, Windows 11, and recent MacOS devices via Endpoint DLP

Some example events gathered from endpoint DLP devices include the following actions taken on files:

- Deletion
- Creation
- Copy to clipboard
- Modify
- Read
- Print
- Rename
- Copy to network share
- Access by an unallowed app

Activity Explorer helps organizations understand users' actions on sensitive labeled content. This can help determine if the policies and controls they have put in place are effective and what may need to be modified or improved.

Sensitivity labels

Microsoft Purview Information Protection sensitivity labels can help organizations discover, classify, and protect sensitive information wherever it lives or travels. Sensitivity labels are core to these activities and have been discussed in the topics earlier in this chapter. Sensitivity labels enable you to classify and protect your organization's data while ensuring that user productivity and their ability to collaborate are not hindered. But what exactly are sensitivity labels?

Sensitivity labels are metadata that are applied to content, which can optionally include visual content markings and encryption of the data itself. This metadata, markings, and encryption are applied directly to the data and follow it wherever it is stored or travels. Sensitivity labels are like a stamp applied to content and are customizable, stored as clear text metadata within files and emails, and are persistent.

Sensitivity labels can be customized to meet the needs of any organization and can be modeled after existing classification schemas. The default sensitivity labels that are created when you create your tenant are **Personal**, **Public**, **General**, **Confidential**, and **Highly Confidential**. These are almost identical to the top-level sensitivity labels used within Microsoft (the exception being **Non-Business** rather than **Personal**). These labels are stored as clear text metadata within files and emails to allow DLP systems to use this information to take actions to prevent sensitive content from being compromised. Storing the labels as metadata inside files and emails allows them to be persistent and roam with the content regardless of where it is saved or stored.

You can use sensitivity labels to

- **Provide protection settings that include encryption and content markings** For example, apply a **Confidential** label to a document or email, and that label encrypts the content and applies a "Confidential" watermark. Content markings include headers and footers as well as watermarks, and encryption can also restrict what actions authorized people can take on the content.

- **Protect content in Office apps across different platforms and devices** Supported by Word, Excel, PowerPoint, and Outlook on the Office desktop apps and Office on the web. Supported on Windows, macOS, iOS, and Android.

- **Protect content in third-party apps and services** With Defender for Cloud apps, you can detect, classify, label, and protect content in third-party apps and services, such as SalesForce, Box, or Dropbox, even if the third-party app or service doesn't read or support sensitivity labels.

- **Protect containers** Including Microsoft Teams, Microsoft 365 Groups, and SharePoint sites. For example, set privacy settings, external user access and external sharing, and access from unmanaged devices.

- **Protect meetings and chat** Label (and optionally encrypt) meeting invites and any responses, and enforce Microsoft Teams–specific options for the meeting and chat.

- **Extend sensitivity labels to Power BI** When you turn on this capability, you can apply and view labels in Power BI and protect data when it's saved outside the service.

- **Extend sensitivity labels to assets in Microsoft Purview Data Map**   When you turn on this capability, currently in preview, you can apply your sensitivity labels to files and schematized data assets in Microsoft Purview Data Map. The schematized data assets include SQL, Azure SQL, Azure Synapse, Azure Cosmos DB, and AWS RDS.

- **Extend sensitivity labels to third-party apps and services**   Using the Microsoft Information Protection SDK, third-party apps can read sensitivity labels and apply protection settings.

- **Label content without using any protection settings**   You can also just apply a label as a result of identifying the sensitivity of the data. This action provides users with a visual mapping of your organization's data sensitivity, and the labels can generate usage reports and activity data for data with different sensitivity levels. Based on this information, you can always apply protection settings later.

- **Protect data when Microsoft Copilot for Microsoft 365 is assigned to users**   Copilot recognizes and integrates sensitivity labels into the user interactions to help keep labeled data protected.

Each file or email may have only one sensitivity label applied at any time. However, you may have both a sensitivity label and a separate retention label applied to the same document. Sensitivity labels can be configured for use with files, emails, applications, and services. Some of the main uses of sensitivity labels include

- **Encryption**   Encryption of emails, meeting invites, and documents to prevent unauthorized people from accessing this data. You can also choose which users or groups have permission to perform which actions and for how long. For example, you can allow all users in your organization to modify a document while a specific group in another organization can only view it. Alternatively, instead of administrator-defined permissions, you can allow your users to assign permissions to the content when they apply the label.

- **Marking the content**   You can mark content using Office apps by adding watermarks, headers, or footers to emails, meeting invites, or documents that have the label applied. Watermarks can be applied to documents but not emails or meeting invites. Dynamic markings are also supported by using variables. For example, you can insert the label name or document name into the header, footer, or watermark.

- **Applying labels automatically**   You can automatically apply labels in Office applications as you work on individual files and services like SharePoint Online and the AIP scanner to apply labels in bulk. You may also set conditions to have Office apps recommend a label based on an email or document's content.

- **Protecting content using containers**   You can protect content using containers when using sensitivity labels with Microsoft Teams, Microsoft 365 groups, and SharePoint sites. Although this configuration does not directly result in the content of these containers inheriting the label and associated protection, the containers use the labels to control access to the location where the content is stored. These settings include privacy settings, external user access, external sharing, and access from unmanaged devices.

Before users, applications, and services can use sensitivity labels, the labels must first be assigned to a label policy. Label policies allow specific users and groups to see the labels published to each policy. Label policies allow administrators to assign a default label that will be applied to all documents and emails created by users of a specific policy. They can also require users to justify changing the label of a document to a lower-ordered label (for instance, changing from **Confidential** to **Public**). Additionally, policies can make labeling of documents and emails mandatory for the in-scope users. This means a user must apply a label before saving a document or sending an email.

Data loss prevention

Organizations regularly handle sensitive information, including financial data, trade secrets, and personal data that is entrusted to them by their users and customers. Protecting this sensitive data and reducing the risk of inappropriate disclosure is often called data loss prevention (DLP).

Microsoft Purview helps organizations implement data loss prevention through DLP policies. These policies enable organizations to identify, monitor, and automatically protect sensitive items across

- Microsoft 365 services such as Teams, Exchange, SharePoint, and OneDrive
- Office applications such as Word, Excel, and PowerPoint
- Windows 10, Windows 11, and recent MacOS endpoints
- Non-Microsoft cloud apps
- On-premises file shares and on-premises SharePoint
- Power BI

DLP detects sensitive items using deep content analysis, not just a simple text scan. Content is analyzed

- For primary data matches to keywords.
- By the evaluation of regular expressions
- By internal function validation
- By secondary data matches that are in proximity to the primary data match.

DLP also uses machine learning algorithms and other methods to detect content that matches your DLP policies.

DLP policies also help users better understand real-time compliance through inline notifications and policy tips. For instance, if a user enters a Social Security number or credit card number in a Microsoft Teams chat, the DLP policy can automatically block the message and notify the user that the policy prevented this.

DLP policies allow organizations to monitor users' activities on sensitive items at rest, in transit, or in use and take protective actions. If a user attempts to take a prohibited action (such as storing sensitive data in unapproved locations or sharing financial information via email), DLP can take one of the following actions:

- Display a policy tip that warns the user that they may be attempting to share sensitive content inappropriately

- Conditionally block the sharing activity and use a policy tip to allow the user to override the block and capture the user's justification

- Fully block the sharing activity with no override option

- When dealing with data at rest, lock the sensitive content and move it to a secure quarantine location

- Prevent the display of sensitive information in Teams chat

To get started protecting data with DLP policies, you must first configure them properly so they will be effective. To configure DLP policies, five questions must be answered:

1. **What data should we monitor?** Microsoft 365 includes predefined policy templates that can assist with identifying sensitive data, including financial data, privacy-related data, and health data. In addition, you may define a custom policy that can identify your organization's sensitive information types, sensitivity labels, or retention labels.

2. **What is the administrative scope?** DLP policies can be assigned to specific administrative units, and the administrators assigned to these units can only create and manage policies for the users, groups, distribution groups, and accounts within that scope.

3. **Where is the data we want to monitor stored?** You must define the locations you want DLP to monitor for sensitive information. These can be any of the previously mentioned locations.

4. **What conditions must apply for the data to be matched by the policy?** Microsoft 365 comes with predefined conditions you can use, or you can define custom conditions that will define a DLP policy match. Some examples include identifying sensitive information types or sensitivity labels and when sensitive information is being shared externally.

5. **What actions will be taken when data is matched to the policy?** Actions that can be taken depend on the location or service where the policy match occurred. For instance, SharePoint, Exchange, and OneDrive allow you to block external parties from accessing the content, whereas when a policy match takes place on on-premises file shares, the matched files are moved to a secure quarantine location.

After you have defined the parameters for your DLP policy, you can implement it within the Microsoft Purview compliance portal. You have a few options for creating DLP policies, and you can use a predefined template and customize it to your needs or create a custom DLP policy. Figure 4-9 shows the policy creation page using a template for identifying HIPPA data.

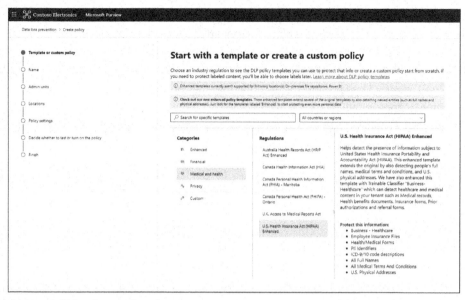

FIGURE 4-9 DLP policy creation page

Endpoint data loss prevention

Microsoft Purview allows you to monitor activities taking place on Windows 10, Windows 11, and macOS devices via Endpoint data loss prevention (Endpoint DLP). You can audit and optionally restrict the following activities using Endpoint DLP:

- Upload of protected items to a cloud service or access by unallowed browsers
- Copying sensitive information from a protected item to another application
- Copying protected items to USB removable media
- Copying protected items to a network share or mapped network drive
- Printing of protected items to a local or network printer
- Copying protected items to a remote desktop session
- Copying protected items to unallowed Bluetooth applications
- Creation of items (audit only)
- Renaming of items (audit only)
- Copying sensitive data to the clipboard
- Accessing protected files by unallowed applications

Endpoint DLP supports the monitoring of the following file types:

- Word files
- PowerPoint files
- Excel files
- ∎ .dlp files
- ∎ .txt files
- ∎ .rtf files

- .pdf files
- .csv files
- .tsv files
- .zip files
- .zipx files
- .rar files
- .7z files
- .tar files
- .war files
- .gz files

- .c files
- .class files
- .cpp files
- .cs files
- .h files
- .java files
- .html files
- .htm files
- .json files
- .config files

Endpoint DLP monitors activity using MIME type, so the activities will still be monitored even if a file extension is changed. The activity recorded by Endpoint DLP is available via the **Alerts** tab in the **Data Loss Prevention** section of the Microsoft Purview compliance portal.

DLP alerts allow you to see the results of DLP policy matches, actions, and user activities. These results are stored in the Microsoft Purview compliance portal Audit Logs and then forwarded to various reporting tools like the DLP Alerts Management dashboard and DLP Activity Explorer. The DLP Alerts Management dashboard allows you to configure and review alerts, triage them in a central location, and track them through resolution. You can filter the alerts within the dashboard by **Time Range**, **User**, **Alert Status**, and **Alert Severity**.

The DLP Activity Explorer operates like the Activity Explorer described in the previous section but has the **Activity** filter preset to DLPRuleMatch. This lets you quickly see all DLP policy matches and filter the activity using the standard filters.

Records management

Most organizations require a records-management solution to manage regulatory, legal, and business-critical records across their data estate. Records management in Microsoft Purview can assist organizations with managing their legal obligations, maintaining compliance with regulations, and increasing efficiency through the regular disposition of items that are no longer required to be retained, no longer of value, or no longer required for business purposes.

Records management in Microsoft Purview provides organizations with capabilities to

- **Label content as a record** Content can be labeled as a record using retention labels applied manually by users or automatically by identifying sensitive information, keywords, or content types.

- **Migrate and manage your retention requirements with a file plan** This allows organizations to bring in an existing retention plan or build a new one for enhanced management capabilities.

- **Configure retention and deletion settings with retention labels** These retention labels can set retention periods and actions based on factors such as the last modified date or creation date.

- **Event-based retention** You can start different retention periods when an event occurs using event-based retention.

- **Review and validate disposition** You can review and validate disposition with disposition reviews and proof of records deletion.

- **Export option** You can export information about all disposed items with the **Export** option.

- **Set specific permissions** You can set specific permissions for Records Manager functions in your organization.

Retention labels can mark content as a record or **regulatory record**. When content is marked as a record, restrictions are placed on the types of actions that are allowed or blocked, additional logging is generated for activities related to the item, and you have proof of disposition after the item is deleted at the end of the retention period. Regulatory records have additional controls, such as preventing the removal of the label from the item and preventing the retention period from being shortened after applying the label.

> **MORE INFO ALLOWABLE AND BLOCKED ACTION**
>
> Additional information about the actions that are allowed and blocked on different types of records can be found at *https://aka.ms/SC900_RecordActions*.

Records management in Microsoft Purview has many common uses. These include the declaration and management of records using retention labels, allowing administrators and users to manually apply labels to set retention and deletion actions on documents and emails, and allowing users to set retention actions automatically using Outlook rules. Organizations can also configure retention periods based on events like employee termination, contract expiration, and end of product lifecycle.

> **MORE INFO RECORDS-MANAGEMENT USE CASES**
>
> Additional use cases for records management in Microsoft Purview can be found at *https://aka.ms/SC900_RMCommonScenarios*.

Retention policies and labels

Today's organizations must manage an ever-growing data estate containing years and even decades of stored information. Retention policies and labels can help ensure that data is kept compliant with regulations, that users are only working with content that is current and relevant to them, and that risk is reduced when dealing with litigation and security breaches.

Organizations can use retention labels and retention policies to

- Proactively comply with internal policies and industry regulations, which require content to be maintained for a minimum amount of time.

- Reduce risk during security breaches or litigation by permanently deleting content that is no longer required to be kept.

- Ensure the content users access is current and relevant, and any outdated or irrelevant data is deleted.

Retention settings work across many Microsoft 365 workloads, including SharePoint and OneDrive sites, Exchange mailboxes and public folders, and Teams and Viva Engage chats and messages. Retention settings are applied to content using retention policies, labels with label policies, or a combination of both.

Retention policies assign uniform retention settings for content at the site or mailbox level. A retention policy can be used to apply specific retention labels to all content on a specific SharePoint site. For instance, if you have a policy that requires all documents in a specific SharePoint site to be retained for three years, you could apply a retention policy to that site. As retention policies apply to a location rather than individual files, retention settings will not follow content if it is moved out of that location. However, if files are moved or deleted, a copy of that content will be kept in secure storage within the location for the remainder of the retention period.

However, retention labels apply retention policies on an item level, such as on an individual folder, document, or email. This means the retention settings will stay with those items regardless of where they travel. When applying a retention label, you can have the retention period begin when the content is labeled or base it on the content's age or last modified date. A default retention label can be set for SharePoint documents, and trainable classifiers can be configured to apply retention labels to matched content. Retention labels also support disposition review for content before it is permanently deleted and can set content as a record so an organization will always have proof of disposition when content is deleted at the end of its retention period.

Retention labels can also be used to augment retention policies. For example, there could be a situation where you have a site with a retention policy of three years but also have content on that site that needs to be retained for five years. In this case, you could use retention labels on the specific content that needs to be retained longer, and that would take precedence.

MORE INFO **RETENTION LABELS AND POLICIES**

Additional information about retention labels and policies can be found at *https://aka.ms/ SC900_RetentionLabelsAndPolicies.*

EXAM TIP

Make sure you understand when using a retention policy is necessary and how it can help organizations govern their data, reduce risk during data breaches, and ensure regulatory compliance.

Microsoft Purview unified data governance

In the always-expanding landscape of organizational data, the constant creation and influx of information and the evolving patterns of data storage and sharing pose an ongoing challenge for security and compliance administrators. Their never-ending task involves the relentless pursuit of discovering, protecting, and governing sensitive data. As the volume of data continues to surge, data consumers face the challenge of navigating an expanding sea of information, often unaware of the diverse data sources available. At the same time, data producers—those entrusted with creating and maintaining information assets—struggle with the complexity and time-consuming nature of documenting those data sources. Crafting and sustaining comprehensive documentation becomes a multifaceted challenge in a dynamic data landscape. A primary aspect of this complexity lies in restricting access to data sources, ensuring that sensitive information is safeguarded, and establishing mechanisms to educate and guide data consumers on the proper channels for requesting access.

Microsoft Purview unified data governance is designed to address the challenges caused by the relentless data growth within organizations. This innovative platform is designed to empower enterprises not only to navigate the complexities of their expanding data estate but also to extract maximum value from it. By addressing the intricacies associated with data growth, Microsoft Purview unified data governance helps organizations seeking to enhance their data governance, security, and compliance measures.

Microsoft Purview unified data governance helps organizations to manage on-premises, multicloud, and Software as a Service (SaaS) data. The Microsoft Purview governance portal allows you to

- Create a holistic, up-to-date map of your data landscape with automated data discovery, sensitive data classification, and end-to-end data lineage.
- Enable data curators and security administrators to manage and secure your data estate.
- Empower data consumers to find valuable, trustworthy data.

We will discuss several key areas shown in Figure 4-10: Data Map, Data Catalog, Data Sharing, Data Estate Insights, and Data Policy.

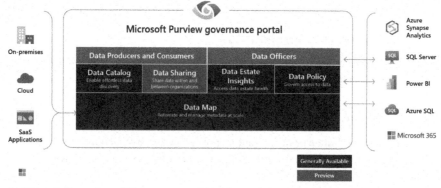

FIGURE 4-10 Illustration of the core areas of the Microsoft Purview governance portal

Data Map

The Microsoft Purview Data Map is the foundation for data discovery and data governance. The Data Map automates data discovery by providing data scanning and classification for assets across your data estate. Metadata containing descriptions of data assets is integrated into a holistic map of your data estate. The gathered metadata is kept up to date using the built-in scanning and classification system. There are two different ways for users to interact with the Data Map; the first is through an intuitive user interface, and the other is to interact programmatically via the open-source Apache Atlas 2.2 APIs. Microsoft Purview supports Azure data sources and various data source categories, including databases, file storage, and applications and services from third parties.

Data Catalog app

The Microsoft Purview Data Catalog app allows business and technical users to quickly and easily find relevant data using a search and browse experience with filters based on various areas, including glossary terms, classifications, and sensitivity labels. The Microsoft Purview Data Catalog provides data curation capabilities that subject matter experts, data stewards, and data officers can use to enrich the metadata and make it more useful to business users. For example, the business glossary can automatically tag assets with relevant glossary terms. Data consumers and producers can also use data lineage to visually trace the path of data assets as they flow through the data estate.

Figure 4-11 shows a complex data lineage flowing to and from an Azure SQL table. This lineage starts with simple text files that flow through Azure Data Factory activities, eventually landing in the Azure SQL table and being exported to many different systems, including SaaS applications like SAP and multicloud resources like Google Looker.

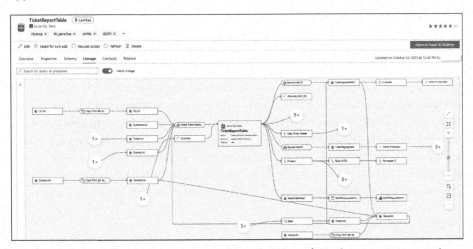

FIGURE 4-11 The data lineage of an Azure SQL table in the Microsoft Purview governance portal

Data Estate Insights app

The Data Estate Insights application is purpose-built for roles focused on data management, compliance, and data use, such as the chief data officer. This application aims to provide actionable insights into the usage, adoption, and processes of the organization's data estate. The Data Estate Insights application automatically extracts valuable governance information while scanning and curating the Data Map. It provides details on gaps and highlights them in its top metrics. This enables stakeholders such as data owners and data stewards to take action to close those gaps.

There are three sections containing dashboards and reports that are available within Microsoft Purview Data Estate Insights:

- **Health**   This section contains the Stewardship Insights report broken down into the Data Estate and Catalog Adoption dashboards. The Stewardship Insights report contains information for users focused on data, governance, and quality, like chief data officers and stewards. This report and associated dashboards help these users understand the health status of their data estate and the current return on investment on their catalog and address any outstanding issues.

- **Inventory and Ownership**   This section summarizes data estate inventory for management and data quality-focused users, like data stewards and data curators. The Assets report summarizes the organization's data estate and asset distribution by source type and collection. This can also identify any new, deleted, updated, or stale assets from the last 30 days.

- **Curation and governance**   This section is focused on how curated the organization's assets are regarding glossary, classification, and sensitivity labels.

Data Sharing app

Microsoft Purview Data Sharing empowers organizations to securely exchange data, facilitating seamless sharing within the organization or extending across organizational boundaries to include business partners and customers. This user-friendly process allows for the effortless sharing or receipt of data with just a few clicks. One of the notable features is the central management and monitoring capabilities afforded to data providers, enabling them to oversee and, if necessary, revoke data-sharing relationships at any given time. This granular control enhances security and compliance measures. On the receiving end, data consumers can access the received data using their preferred analytics tools, enabling them to translate raw data into valuable insights. This robust and versatile data-sharing framework is designed to streamline collaboration and empower organizations to derive maximum value from their data assets.

Data Policy app

The Microsoft Purview Data Policy application represents a comprehensive set of central, cloud-based functionalities designed to adeptly manage access to data sources and datasets with a strong emphasis on security and scalability. The Microsoft Purview Data Policy application allows for the streamlined administration of access to data sources through a unified, cloud-based interface. This facilitates at-scale access provisioning, simplifying the complex task of managing permissions across many data sources.

Microsoft Purview Data Policy introduces a new data-plane permission model that operates independently of the data sources. This innovative approach enhances flexibility and control, providing a robust foundation for secure data management practices. Seamless integration with the Microsoft Purview Data Map and Catalog adds an extra layer of efficiency to the data governance process. Users can effortlessly search for data assets and employ fine-grained policies to grant access only to what is necessary. This approach aligns with the principle of least privilege, ensuring that users can access only what is required for their tasks. The Microsoft Purview Data Policy application is not confined to a specific data environment; it supports a range of data sources, including SaaS, on-premises, and multicloud configurations. Its ability to leverage metadata associated with the data objects enhances policy creation. Role definitions within the Microsoft Purview Data Policy application are intentionally kept simple and abstracted. For example, roles such as Read and Modify are defined to promote clarity and ease of use.

> **MORE INFO** **MICROSOFT PURVIEW UNIFIED DATA GOVERNANCE**
>
> For additional information on Microsoft Purview unified data governance, see the documentation at *https://aka.ms/SC900_PurviewDataGovernance*.

Skill 4.4: Insider risk, eDiscovery, and auditing

Organizations must identify and mitigate many types of risks to protect their information. These risks often come from outside sources but also from insiders like employees and contractors. Protecting your organization against these risks can be challenging to identify and mitigate. In addition, organizations may need to identify, collect, and audit data for regulatory, legal, or business reasons. This section covers the skills necessary to describe the various capabilities of Microsoft Insider Risk Management, eDiscovery, and audit management solutions according to the Exam SC-900 outline.

This skill covers how to:

- Use Microsoft Insider Risk Management to minimize risks by detecting risky or malicious activities and taking action on them
- Use eDiscovery to search for content in Exchange Online, Microsoft 365 Groups, SharePoint Online, OneDrive for Business sites, Microsoft Teams, and Yammer teams
- Quickly search through existing content across Microsoft 365 locations using Content Search

- Search for and export content from Microsoft 365 and Office 365 services via eDiscovery (Standard) workflow
- Understand the additional capabilities available using eDiscovery (Premium) Workflow
- Describe the content available via the unified Audit log
- Describe audit capabilities available via Audit (Standard)
- Understand additional capabilities available using Audit (Premium)

Insider Risk Management

Understanding the types of risks found in the modern workplace should be the first step toward managing and minimizing risk to your organization. Microsoft Purview Insider Risk Management is a solution that aims to minimize risks originating from internal sources by facilitating the detection of risky or malicious activities and allowing you to investigate and act upon them. Some of these risky behaviors include leakage of sensitive data and data spillage, confidentiality violations, intellectual property theft, fraud, insider trading, and regulatory compliance violations. Insider Risk Management is centered around the following principles:

- **Transparency** Balance user privacy versus organization risk with privacy-by-design architecture
- **Configurable** Configurable policies based on industry, geographical, and business groups
- **Integrated** Integrated workflow across Microsoft 365 compliance solutions
- **Actionable** Provides insights to enable reviewer notifications, data investigations, and user investigations

EXAM TIP

Make sure you know and understand the principles of Insider Risk Management.

Insider Risk Management uses a five-step workflow to help organizations identify, investigate, and take remedial action on internal risks. Using policy templates, in-depth activity signaling, and alert and case management tools, organizations can use actionable insights to quickly identify and act on any identified at-risk behavior. The following Insider Risk Management workflow can help to identify and resolve compliance issues and internal risk activities:

- **Policies** Insider Risk Management policies are created using pre defined templates and policy conditions that define what risk indicators will be evaluated. Some of these conditions include how risk indicators are used for alerts, what users are included, which services are prioritized, and the effective period. There are many pre defined policy templates you can choose from to get started:

- Data theft by departing users
- General data leaks
- Data leaks by priority users (preview)
- Data leaks by risky users (preview)
- Security policy violations (preview)
- Security policy violations by departing users (preview)
- Security policy violations by priority users (preview)
- Security policy violations by risky users (preview)
- Patient data misuse (preview)
- Risky browser usage (preview)

- **Alerts**   When risk indicators that match policy conditions are found, alerts are automatically generated and displayed within the **Alerts** dashboard in the **Insider Risk** section of the Microsoft Purview compliance portal. This dashboard shows a prioritized list of alerts needing review, categorizing them as high, medium, and low severity. Policy alerts are displayed with the following information to help you quickly identify the status of existing alerts and new alerts that need action:

  - ID
  - Users
  - Alert
  - Status
  - Alert severity
  - Time detected
  - Case
  - Case status
  - Risk factors

- **Triage**   When new activities that need investigation are identified, they are placed in a **Needs Review** status. This helps reviewers to review and triage these alerts quickly. To resolve alerts in this status, reviewers can open a new case, assign the alert to an existing case, or dismiss the alert. Alert filters can quickly sort alerts by time detected, status, or severity. During the triage process, reviewers can view details of the identified activity, view user activity associated with the policy match, review the alert severity, and see additional user profile details.

- **Investigate**   Once an alert that requires additional investigation is identified during the triage phase, a case is created. The Case dashboard provides a view of all currently active cases, open cases over time, and additional case statistics. When a case is selected from the dashboard, it will be opened for investigation and review. This is the most important step in the Insider Risk Management workflow. Reviewers can see each case's alert details, matched policy conditions, risk activities, and related user details. The investigation tools available in this area include User Activity, Content Explorer, and a section to provide case notes.

- **Action**   Once cases have been investigated, the final step in the workflow is to act on the findings. Reviewers can resolve the case or collaborate with other stakeholders in the organization. If the action was unintentional, the resolution could be as simple as sending a reminder notice to the user or directing them to additional compliance training. If the situation is more serious, you may need to share information related to the case with other stakeholders in the organization.

There are many common scenarios where Insider Risk Management can help organizations detect, investigate, and take corrective action. Some of these include the intentional or unintentional leak of sensitive information, security policy violations, data theft by departing employees, actions taken by risky employees, and general offensive behavior.

eDiscovery

Electronic discovery (eDiscovery) involves identifying and delivering electronic information that can be used as evidence in legal cases. The eDiscovery tools in Microsoft 365 can be used to search for content in Exchange Online, Microsoft 365 Groups, SharePoint Online, OneDrive for Business sites, Microsoft Teams, and Yammer teams. There are three primary components to eDiscovery: Content Search, eDiscovery (Standard), and eDiscovery (Premium).

Content across Microsoft 365 data sources can be searched in a single eDiscovery query by using the Content Search tool. eDiscovery (Standard) cases can be used to identify, hold, and export content from sites and mailboxes. eDiscovery (Premium) is part of the Office 365 E5 or Microsoft 365 E5 subscription (or related E5 add-on subscriptions) and allows you to manage custodians further and analyze content.

Content search

The Content Search tool available in the Microsoft Purview compliance portal can quickly search through existing content across SharePoint sites and OneDrive locations, Exchange Online mailboxes, and conversations in Microsoft Teams, Microsoft 365, and Yammer groups.

The first thing you must do to use Content Search is create a new search query. This consists of a meaningful name, the content location you would like to search, and any keywords and additional conditions you would like to search on. Figure 4-12 shows the new search conditions page.

FIGURE 4-12 New search condition page in the Content Search function

You may also leave the keywords and conditions blank in the search query to return all content from the selected location(s). After you run a query, it returns matched content, and there are several options for actions you can take with that data. Following are some examples of actions you can take on the search results:

- **Export the results**   This allows you to download the matched content results to your computer for additional analysis.

- **Search for and delete email messages**   This action can allow you to delete malicious content like viruses and phishing messages.

- **Export a report**   You can also export a summary of the content found for reporting purposes without exporting any actual content.

To perform these actions, you can select a search query in the **Content Search** section of the Microsoft Purview compliance portal and click the **Actions** button at the bottom of the **Search** tab, as shown in Figure 4-13.

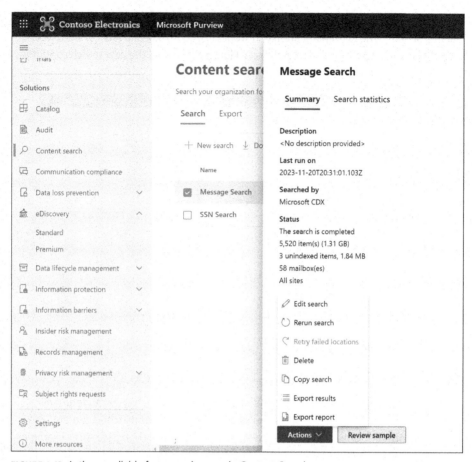

FIGURE 4-13 Actions available for a search query in Content Search

eDiscovery (Standard) Workflow

eDiscovery (Standard) in Microsoft Purview allows organizations to search for and export content from Microsoft 365 and Office 365 services. You may also use eDiscovery (Standard) in places like SharePoint sites, OneDrive accounts, Exchange mailboxes, and Microsoft Teams to place an eDiscovery hold on specific items. Although eDiscovery (Standard) is enabled by default, three enterprise apps must be enabled to access the eDiscovery (Standard) view, filter, and search filters to use the functionality. These are identified in Table 4-2.

TABLE 4-2 eDiscovery (Standard) Enterprise Apps

App	App ID
ComplianceWorkbenchApp	92876b03-76a3-4da8-ad6a-0511ffdf8647
Microsoft Exchange Online Protection	00000007-0000-0ff1-ce00-000000000000
Office365Zoom	0d38933a-0bbd-41ca-9ebd-28c4b5ba7cb7

In addition to enabling these apps, a user must be a member of the eDiscovery Manager role group in the Microsoft Purview compliance portal to use eDiscovery (Standard).

After assigning appropriate permissions, you may create new eDiscovery cases by going to the **eDiscovery > Standard** page in the Microsoft Purview compliance portal. The only requirement to create a new case is to give it a case name that is unique to your organization. You may optionally add additional case information and members to the case on the Settings tab within the case, as shown in Figure 4-14.

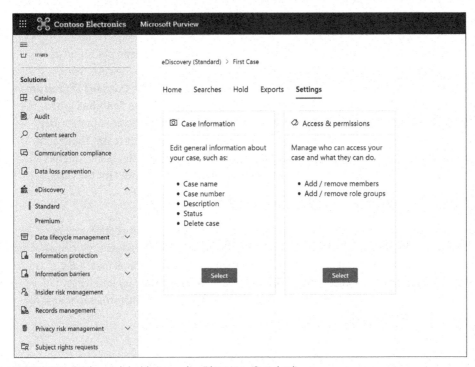

FIGURE 4-14 Settings tab inside a case in eDiscovery (Standard)

After creating a new case, you can step through the eDiscovery (Standard) workflow, which consists of three steps: creating an eDiscovery hold, searching for content, and exporting content.

Create an eDiscovery hold

eDiscovery (Standard) cases can be used to preserve content relevant to a case by creating eDiscovery holds. Holds may be placed on content in mailboxes and sites associated with Microsoft Teams and Microsoft 365 Groups. When these locations are placed on hold, the content is preserved until you have removed or deleted the hold on the location. eDiscovery holds can take up to 24 hours before they take effect.

When an eDiscovery hold is created, there are two options available to scope the content that will be preserved in the designated locations:

- **Create An Infinite Hold**   When this type of hold is created, all content in the designated location is placed on hold. A query may also be used to scope down to a smaller subset of data in that location.

- **Specify A Date Range**   This allows you to place a hold on only data created, sent, or received during the specified date range.

Search for content in a case

Once the eDiscovery (Standard) case has been created and a hold has been placed on designated locations, you can run searches on the content that is related to the case. Searches related to eDiscovery cases are not listed under the search queries in the **Content Search** area in the Microsoft Purview compliance portal. Rather, they are listed on the **Searches** tab for the specific case for which the searches were created. This prevents users who are not members of a specific case from seeing what searches are taking place related to the case. The search queries created under an eDiscovery (Standard) case are very similar to the search queries in Content Search except that they can specifically target areas placed on hold for the case.

Export content from a case

You can export the search results after successfully running a search query within a case. When search results are exported from SharePoint and OneDrive for Business sites, copies of the documents will be exported. The items will be downloaded as individual messages or as PST files for mailbox content. In addition to the individual items, a summary Results.csv file is exported with information about each of the exported items, and an XML format manifest file is created with information about each search result.

Additional actions

Once you have completed a case, there are a few additional actions that can take place as part of the eDiscovery (Standard) lifecycle:

- **Upgrade a case to eDiscovery (Premium)**   There are times when working with eDiscovery (Standard) cases that you may need the additional functionality provided by eDiscovery (Premium). This functionality is now available, but several items need to be understood before upgrading to an eDiscovery (Premium) case:
  - After an eDiscovery (Standard) case is upgraded to eDiscovery (Premium), it can't be reversed to an eDiscovery (Standard) case.
  - Only eDiscovery Administrators can upgrade cases to eDiscovery (Premium).
  - Search changes aren't available while the case is upgrading to eDiscovery (Premium). Once a case is upgraded, searches are available under the Collections section in the eDiscovery (Premium) case.

- Information for jobs created in the eDiscovery (Standard) case is maintained after the upgrade, though the job names retain the eDiscovery (Standard) case job names.

- Holds in the Standard case are maintained in the upgraded Premium case. No holds are removed or recreated during the upgrade process. This ensures that holds aren't lost or deleted during the upgrade.

- The eDiscovery (Standard) case search conditions are copied to a new eDiscovery (Premium) case collection. You can refresh/rerun the estimates, though this replaces all previous search statistics for the search.

- **Close a case**   When the investigation or legal case that eDiscovery (Standard) was used for is complete, you may close the case. After the case is closed, all related eDiscovery holds will be disabled, and a 30-day grace period (delay hold) will be placed on the content to prevent it from being immediately deleted. This gives the case admin time to search and restore content before permanently deleting it. Although the case is closed, it will remain on the eDiscovery (Standard) page in the compliance portal, and all details related to the case (holds, members, searches) will be retained.

- **Reopen a case**   There may be instances where cases must be reopened after they are closed. Because all the details are retained, this can be done easily from the eDiscovery (Standard) page. When a case is reopened, the holds are not immediately reinstated and must be turned on manually from the hold tab.

- **Delete a case**   Both active and closed cases can be deleted. Deleting a case is different from simply closing the case, as all details, searches, holds, and members are lost, and the case is removed from the list of cases on the eDiscovery (Standard) page.

eDiscovery (Premium) workflow

eDiscovery (Premium) builds on top of the existing Microsoft eDiscovery (Standard) capabilities by adding an end-to-end workflow to identify, preserve, collect, process, review, analyze, and export content relevant to your organization's investigations. It also allows for close collaboration between legal teams and case custodians and allows them to manage the legal hold notifications. To use the functionality of eDiscovery (Premium), four enterprise apps must be enabled to access the eDiscovery (Premium) view, filter, and search features. These are identified in Table 4-3.

TABLE 4-3 eDiscovery (Premium) Enterprise Apps

App	App ID
ComplianceWorkbenchApp	92876b03-76a3-4da8-ad6a-0511ffdf8647
MicrosoftPurviewEDiscovery	b26e684c-5068-4120-a679-64a5d2c909d9
Microsoft Exchange Online Protection	00000007-0000-0ff1-ce00-000000000000
Office365Zoom	0d38933a-0bbd-41ca-9ebd-28c4b5ba7cb7

The eDiscovery (Premium) workflow was designed to align with the Electronic Discovery Reference Model (EDRM), a framework outlining standards for recovering and discovering digital data. The five steps of the eDiscovery (Premium) workflow include

- **Identify**   The first step in the eDiscovery (Premium) is to identify persons of interest and add them as custodians/data custodians because they may have relevant information to the case.

- **Preserve**   The next step is to gather additional data sources relevant to the case that are not associated with specific users. This data (and custodian data) is then reindexed, and a hold may be placed on the data to preserve relevant case information. The communication workflow in eDiscovery (Premium) can be used to send legal hold notifications and track user acknowledgment.

- **Collect**   Once custodians and non custodial data sources have been added to the case, the built-in eDiscovery (Premium) tool may be used to search and collect relevant data from these data sources.

- **Process**   After you've collected all data relevant to the case, the next step is to process it for further review and analysis.

- **Review**   Once the search has been run and you have verified that it has collected the data you are looking for, you can add the results to a review set. You also can view specific documents and run additional queries to reduce the data to what is most relevant to the case. You can also annotate and tag specific documents.

- **Analyze**   Once the data is in the review set, you can analyze the case data and reduce it to what is most relevant. Several tools can be used, including viewing documents, using queries and filters (including metadata properties), applying tags to the items, annotating and redacting specific information, and using the analytics functionality of eDiscovery (Premium).

- **Produce and Present**   The final step is to export the data from eDiscovery (Premium) for legal review. You can export documents in their native format or in an EDRM-specified format to be imported into third-party review applications.

Auditing

The Microsoft Purview compliance portal has auditing ability, allowing organizations to view user and administrator activity via a unified Audit Log. This Audit Log allows compliance administrators and auditors to identify changes that have taken place throughout the Microsoft 365 ecosystem. This can include locations like the core Microsoft 365 services such as SharePoint Online, Exchange Online, OneDrive, and Teams but also extends to additional applications and services like Azure Active Directory, Microsoft Power Apps, PowerBI, Dynamics 365, and others.

MORE INFO   **UNIFIED AUDIT LOG**

A full list of locations and activities that can be monitored via the unified Audit Log can be found at *https://aka.ms/SC900_AuditActivities*.

Two auditing types are available in Microsoft Purview depending on the license assigned to specific users: Audit (Standard) and Audit (Premium).

Microsoft Purview Audit capabilities

Microsoft Purview allows organizations to monitor activities performed by users and administrators via the unified Audit Log. In most Microsoft 365 organizations, Audit (Standard) is enabled by default. When an audited activity is performed, an audit record is generated and stored in the unified Audit Log. With Audit (Standard), these records are retained and may be searched for up to 180 days.

Two roles may be assigned to allow users to access and search the Audit Log: View-Only Audit Logs and Audit Logs. Users can search the unified Audit Log once the role has been assigned to them. Four criteria may be used to filter search results in the classic search. These are shown in Figure 4-15.

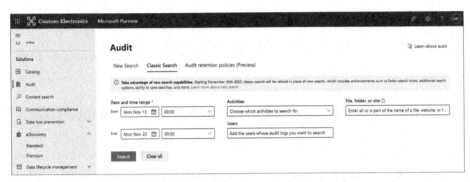

FIGURE 4-15 Content Explorer in the Microsoft Purview compliance portal

- The **Date And Time Range** setting allows you to narrow the search scope to a specific timeframe, shown in your local time. The search will default to show the last seven days of audited activity.

- The **Activities** setting allows you to define specific audited activities you want to include in the search. Leaving this blank will return all audited activities during the specified timeframe.

- The **File, Folder, Or Site** setting allows you to provide a specific keyword to narrow the search. As with activities, this can be left blank to return all audited locations.

- The **Users** setting allows you to narrow your search results by selecting specific users. This search box will perform an Entra ID lookup as you type to help quickly select the users or service accounts you are interested in finding.

The search results will initially show up to 150 items but will dynamically increase as you scroll through them. As shown in Figure 4-16, you can export a CSV of all search results by using the **Export** button.

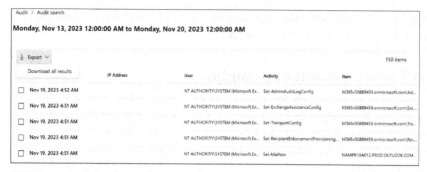

FIGURE 4-16 Audit Log Search Results can be exported to CSV using the Export > Download all results button

The Audit Log Search returns the following information for each audit entry:

- **Date**   The event is recorded and shown in your local time.
- **IP Address**   Either IPv4 or IPv6 format from the device used when the activity was recorded.
- **User**   The user (or service account) that performed the action that triggered the audit entry.
- **Activity**   The activity that was performed.
- **Item**   The item created or modified based on the activity (not all activities will contain values in this column).
- **Detail**   Detail related to the activity (not all activities will contain values in this column).

In addition to this basic information, you can click each **Audit Log Search Results** entry to see the **Details** pane, as shown in Figure 4-17.

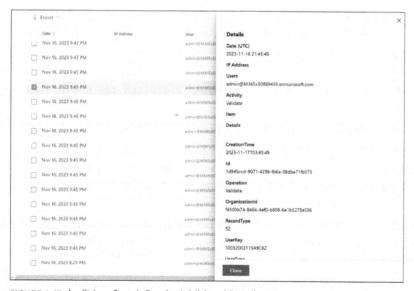

FIGURE 4-17 Audit Log Search Results Additional Details pane

Audit (Premium)

While Audit (Standard) in Microsoft Purview is an amazing tool for monitoring and compliance, additional capabilities are available via Audit (Premium) in Microsoft 365. Audit (Premium) expands on the capabilities of Audit (Standard) by increasing Audit Log retention to facilitate the longer timeframes needed to conduct forensic and compliance investigations, providing access to additional events that could prove crucial for determining the scope of a compromise and allowing direct, high-bandwidth access to the Office 365 Management Activity API.

Audit (Premium) is available to organizations with a Microsoft 365 Enterprise or Office 365 E5/A5/G5 subscription. Organizations with Microsoft 365/Office 365 E3 licenses may also use Audit (Premium) capabilities with either a Microsoft 365 E5 Compliance or Microsoft 365 E5 eDiscovery and Audit add-on license.

Audit (Premium) retains all Exchange, SharePoint, and Azure Active Directory audit records for a full year. Audit records can be maintained for as long as 10 years with an additional add-on license. Retaining these logs for 10 years can help support long-running investigations and respond to regulatory, legal, and internal obligations. The default Audit Log retention policy retains the abovementioned workloads for one year and all other services for 90 days. You may optionally create custom Audit Log retention policies to retain other types of audit records for periods of up to 10 years. These policies can be configured to target specific Microsoft 365 services where audited activities occur, specified audit activities, or specific users who perform audited activities.

Access to crucial events for investigations

Audit (Premium) can also help organizations conduct forensic and compliance investigations by providing advanced details like when mail items were accessed, the time and content of searches conducted in SharePoint Online and Exchange Online, and when mail items were forwarded or replied to. These items can assist with investigations of potential breaches and help evaluate the scope of a compromise. Specifically, Audit (Premium) provides access to the following crucial events:

- **MailItemsAccessed**   This event is a mailbox audit action that triggers mail data accessed by mail protocols or mail clients. This event can help investigators identify when there has been a data breach and determine the scope of messages that may have been compromised.

- **Send**   The send event is another mailbox audit event triggered when a user sends, replies to, or forwards an email message. This event can help investigators identify details around email messages sent by an attacker or from a compromised account. These events contain details, including when the message was sent, if it included any attachments, the subject line, and the InternetMessage ID. Investigators can use the subject line or message ID from this event to find where the message was sent and identify other potentially compromised accounts using eDiscovery tools.

- **SearchQueryInitiatedExchange**   This event is triggered when a user searches for items in a mailbox using an Outlook desktop or mobile client, Outlook on the web

(OWA), or the Windows 10 Mail app. Investigators can use this to determine if an attacker attempted to access sensitive information in a compromised mailbox. This event contains the full text of the search query and can help investigators better understand what information an attacker may be targeting.

- **SearchQueryInitiatedSharePoint** This event is similar to the previous one but is triggered when a search occurs on a SharePoint site. This event can help investigators determine what an attacker was searching for and potentially identify sensitive information in SharePoint that the attacker accessed. This event also contains the full text of the search query and can help understand what information is being targeted by the attacker.

- **Other Audit (Premium) events** Other Microsoft 365 services also provide Audit (Premium) events. Some of these services are

  - Microsoft Forms
  - Microsoft Stream
  - Microsoft Project for the web
  - Microsoft Teams
  - Microsoft To Do
  - Viva Engage

In addition to access to crucial events, Audit (Premium) also gives organizations high-bandwidth access to the Office 365 management API. In the past, API access to Audit Logs was restricted by throttling limits placed at the publisher level. With the release of Audit (Premium), Microsoft has changed from a publisher-level limit to a tenant-level limit, providing each organization with its allocated bandwidth quota for accessing audit data. This quota scales with the number of licenses an organization purchases and the type of license. Organizations with E5 licenses will receive around twice the amount of bandwidth as non-E5 organizations.

Thought experiment

In this thought experiment, demonstrate your skills and knowledge of the topics covered in this chapter. You can find answers to this thought experiment in the next section.

Protecting Contoso's Data Estate

You are a compliance admin working for Contoso Electronics, a multinational corporation that provides specialized electronic components for large computer manufacturers. You have recently migrated many of your on-premises services and workloads to the cloud, and users have been fully onboarded to Exchange Online, SharePoint Online, OneDrive, and Microsoft Teams. This has greatly increased your productivity but has also brought in new risks.

Contoso has encouraged migration of workloads from on-premises systems to the cloud, resulting in an unknown number of structured data sources and unstructured data being onboarded into Azure SQL Server, Synapse Analytics, Azure Data Lake Storage, Azure Blob Storage, and AWS S3 storage locations. The CIO has tasked you with enacting a data governance program to bring the organization's data estate under management and identify where sensitive data is stored, regardless of whether it is unstructured or structured data. Contoso has recently purchased a Microsoft 365 E5 subscription to ensure they can put the best protection for their sensitive data.

With this information in mind, answer the following questions:

1. What can be used to scan cloud data sources to visualize the organization's data estate, classify and label both structured and unstructured analytical data in the cloud, and see full lineage showing where data travels?

2. Beyond just the analytical data stored in the cloud, Contoso has a large amount of unstructured data stored in Microsoft 365 services such as Exchange, SharePoint, and Teams. What is the best way to identify and visualize sensitive data labeled or classified in these services?

3. Your CIO is also concerned with potential risks when employees leave the company or other potential threats resulting in data leakage. What can be done to ensure that data stays secure from bad actors?

Thought experiment answers

This section contains the solution to the thought experiment.

1. Microsoft Purview unified data governance can create a holistic, up-to-date map of your data landscape (Data Map) with automated data discovery, sensitive data classification and labeling, and end-to-end data lineage.

2. You can use Content Explorer to show a consolidated view of data with a sensitivity label assigned or classified as a sensitive information type for your organization.

3. Using Microsoft Purview Insider Risk Management will allow you to minimize risks originating from internal sources by facilitating the detection of risky or malicious activities and allowing you to investigate and act upon them.

Chapter summary

- Microsoft's Service Trust Portal (STP) contains useful content related to
  - Certifications, regulations, and standards
  - Reports, whitepapers, and artifacts

- Industry and regional resources
- Resources for your organization

- The STP also contains a feature known as My Library, which allows you to track specific documents or series of documents and be notified when they change.

- Microsoft's approach to privacy is built on six principles. These are control, transparency, security, strong legal protections, no content-based targeting, and benefits to you.

- Microsoft Priva is a comprehensive solution essential to addressing common challenges like employee training, risk assessments, and data subject requests.

- Compliance Manager provides step-by-step guidance to assist organizations with implementing regulatory requirements and helps to translate complicated regulations into simple language.

- The four key elements of Compliance Manager are Controls, Assessments, Templates, and Improvement Actions.

- **Compliance Score** is initially based on the Microsoft 365 data protection baseline.

- Scores assigned to various actions affect **Compliance Score** based on whether they are mandatory or discretionary and if they are preventative, detective, or corrective actions. Actions that are mandatory and preventative have the highest score value.

- Sensitive information types can be used to identify sensitive information based on specific keywords, functions, or regular expressions.

- Creating a custom trainable classifier requires you to provide between 50 and 500 samples of data that are positive matches for the category. After the samples are processed, a prediction model will be created, and you can test the classifier.

- Content Explorer shows a consolidated view of data with a sensitivity or retention label assigned or classified as a sensitive information type for your organization.

- Activity Explorer supplements the functionality of Content Explorer by showing what activities have occurred on labeled content over time.

- Activity Explorer uses the Microsoft 365 Audit Logs to gather labeling activity information.

- Sensitivity labels are metadata that are applied to content, which can optionally include visual content markings and encryption of the data itself.

- Sensitivity labels are like a stamp applied to content and are customizable, stored as clear text metadata within files and emails, and persistent.

- Retention settings work across SharePoint and OneDrive sites, Exchange mailboxes and public folders, and Teams chats and messages. Retention settings are applied to content using retention policies, labels with label policies, or a combination of both.

- When content is marked as a record, restrictions are put in place on the types of actions that are allowed or blocked, additional logging is generated for activities related to the item, and you have proof of disposition after the item is deleted at the end of the retention period.

■ Regulatory records have additional controls, such as preventing the removal of the label from the item and preventing the retention period from being shortened after applying the label.

■ Microsoft Purview unified data governance helps organizations to manage on-premises, multicloud, and Software as a Service (SaaS) data.

■ The Microsoft Purview governance portal allows you to

  ■ Create a holistic, up-to-date map of your data landscape with automated data discovery, sensitive data classification, and end-to-end data lineage.

  ■ Enable data curators and security administrators to manage and secure your data estate.

  ■ Empower data consumers to find valuable, trustworthy data.

■ Insider Risk Management is centered around the following principles: Transparency, Configurable policies, Integrated workflow, and Actionable insights.

■ Insider Risk Management policies are created using pre defined templates and policy conditions that define what risk indicators will be evaluated.

■ The eDiscovery (Standard) workflow consists of three steps: creating an eDiscovery hold, searching for content, and exporting content.

■ eDiscovery (Premium) builds on top of the existing Microsoft eDiscovery (Standard) capabilities by adding an end-to-end workflow to identify, preserve, collect, process, review, analyze, produce, and present content.

■ Audit (Premium) increases Audit Log retention (up to 10 years), provides access to additional events, and allows high-bandwidth access to the Office 365 Management Activity API.

CHAPTER 5

SC-900 Microsoft Security, Compliance, and Identity Fundamentals exam updates

The purpose of this chapter

For all the other chapters, the content should remain unchanged throughout this edition of the book. However this chapter will change over time, with an updated online PDF posted so you can see the latest version of the chapter, even after you purchase this book.

Why do we need a chapter that updates over time? For three reasons.

1. To add more technical content to the book before it is time to replace the current book edition with the next edition. This chapter includes additional technology content and possibly additional PDFs containing more content.

2. To communicate details about the next exam version, tell you about our publishing plans for that edition, and help you understand what that means to you.

3. To accurately map the current exam objectives to existing chapter content. While exam objectives evolve and are updated and products are renamed, much of the content in this book will remain accurate and relevant. In addition to covering any content gaps that appear through additions to the objectives, this chapter will provide explanatory notes on how the new objectives map to the current text.

After the initial publication of this book, Microsoft Press will provide supplemental updates as digital downloads for minor exam updates. If an exam has major changes or accumulates enough minor changes, we will then announce a new edition. We will do our best to provide any updates to you free of charge before we release a new edition. However, if the updates are significant enough in between editions, we may release the updates as a low-priced standalone eBook.

If we do produce a free updated version of this chapter, you can access it on the book's product page, simply visit *MicrosoftPressStore.com/ERSC9002e/downloads* to view and download the updated material.

About possible exam updates

Microsoft reviews exam content periodically to ensure that it aligns with the technology and job role associated with the exam. This includes (but is not limited to) incorporating functionality and features related to technology changes, changing skills needed for success within a job role, and revisions to product names. Microsoft updates the exam details page to notify candidates when changes occur. If you have registered this book and an update occurs to this chapter, Microsoft Press will notify you of the availability of this updated chapter.

Impact on you and your study plan

Microsoft's information helps you plan, but it also means that the exam might change before you pass the current exam. That impacts you, affecting how we deliver this book to you. This chapter gives us a way to communicate in detail about those changes as they occur. But you should watch other spaces as well.

For other information sources to watch, bookmark and check these sites for news. In particular,

- **Microsoft Learn**   Check the main source for up-to-date information: *microsoft.com/ learn*. Make sure to sign up for automatic notifications from on that page.
- **Microsoft Press**   Find information about products, offers, discounts, and free downloads: *microsoftpressstore.com*. Make sure to register your purchased products.

As changes arise, we will update this chapter with more details about the exam and book content. At that point, we will publish an updated version of this chapter, listing our content plans. That detail will likely include the following:

- Content is removed, so if you plan to take the new exam version, you can ignore that when studying.
- New content is planned per new exam topics, so you know what's coming.

The remainder of the chapter shows the new content that may change over time.

News and commentary about the exam objective updates

- The current official Microsoft Study Guide for the SC-900: Microsoft Security, Compliance, and Identity Fundamentals exam is located at *https://learn.microsoft.com/en-us/ credentials/certifications/exams/sc-900/*. This page has the most recent version of the exam objective domain.
- This statement was last updated in January 2024, before the publication of *Exam Ref SC-900: Microsoft Security, Compliance, and Identity Fundamentals*.
- This version of this chapter has no news to share about the next exam release.

- When the most recent version of this chapter was published, the SC-900: Microsoft Security, Compliance, and Identity Fundamentals exam version number was Version 1.1.

Updated technical content

The current version of this chapter has no additional technical content.

Objective mapping

This *Exam Ref* is structured by the author(s) based on the topics and technologies covered on the exam and not based on the specific order of topics in the exam objectives. Table 5-1 maps the current version of the exam objectives to chapter content, allowing you to locate where a specific exam objective item has coverage without consulting the index.

TABLE 5.1 Exam Objectives mapped to chapters.

Exam Objective	Chapter
Describe the concepts of security, compliance, and identity (10–15%)	
Describe security and compliance concepts	1
■ Describe the shared responsibility model	
■ Describe defense-in-depth	
■ Describe the Zero Trust model	
■ Describe encryption and hashing	
■ Describe Governance, Risk, and Compliance (GRC) concepts	
Define identity concepts	
■ Define identity as the primary security perimeter	
■ Define authentication	
■ Define authorization	
■ Describe identity providers	
■ Describe the concept of directory services and Active Directory	
■ Describe the concept of federation	
Describe the capabilities of Microsoft Entra (25–30%)	
Describe function and identity types of Microsoft Entra ID	2
■ Describe Microsoft Entra ID	
■ Describe types of identities	
■ Describe hybrid identity	
Describe authentication capabilities of Microsoft Entra ID	
■ Describe the authentication methods	
■ Describe multi factor authentication (MFA)	
■ Describe password protection and management capabilities	

Exam Objective	Chapter

Describe access management capabilities of Microsoft Entra ID

- Describe Conditional Access
- Describe Microsoft Entra roles and role-based access control (RBAC)

Describe identity protection and governance capabilities of Microsoft Entra

- Describe Microsoft Entra ID Governance
- Describe access reviews
- Describe the capabilities of Microsoft Entra Privileged Identity Management
- Describe Entra ID Protection
- Describe Microsoft Entra Permissions Management

Describe the capabilities of Microsoft security solutions (35–40%)

Describe core infrastructure security services in Azure   3

- Describe Azure distributed denial-of-service (DDoS) Protection
- Describe Azure Firewall
- Describe Web Application Firewall (WAF)
- Describe network segmentation with Azure virtual networks
- Describe network security groups (NSGs)
- Describe Azure Bastion
- Describe Azure Key Vault

Describe security management capabilities of Azure

- Describe Microsoft Defender for Cloud
- Describe Cloud Security Posture Management (CSPM)
- Describe how security policies and initiatives improve the cloud security posture
- Describe enhanced security features provided by cloud workload protection

Describe capabilities of Microsoft Sentinel

- Define the concepts of security information and event management (SIEM) and security orchestration automated response (SOAR)
- Describe threat detection and mitigation capabilities in Microsoft Sentinel

Describe threat protection with Microsoft 365 Defender

- Describe Microsoft 365 Defender services
- Describe Microsoft Defender for Office 365
- Describe Microsoft Defender for Endpoint
- Describe Microsoft Defender for Cloud Apps

- Describe Microsoft Defender for Identity
- Describe Microsoft Defender Vulnerability Management
- Describe Microsoft Defender Threat Intelligence (Defender TI)
- Describe the Microsoft 365 Defender portal

Exam Objective	Chapter
Describe the capabilities of Microsoft compliance solutions (20–25%)	

Describe Microsoft Service Trust Portal and privacy principles   4

- Describe the Service Trust Portal offerings
- Describe the privacy principles of Microsoft
- Describe Microsoft Priva

Describe compliance management capabilities of Microsoft Purview

- Describe the Microsoft Purview compliance portal
- Describe Compliance Manager
- Describe the uses and benefits of compliance score

Describe information protection, data lifecycle management, and data governance capabilities of Microsoft Purview

- Describe the data classification capabilities
- Describe the benefits of Content Explorer and Activity Explorer
- Describe sensitivity labels and sensitivity label policies
- Describe data loss prevention (DLP)
- Describe records management
- Describe retention policies, retention labels, and retention label policies
- Describe unified data governance solutions in Microsoft Purview

Describe insider risk, eDiscovery, and audit capabilities in Microsoft Purview

- Describe insider risk management
- Describe eDiscovery solutions in Microsoft Purview
- Describe audit solutions in Microsoft Purview

Index